The Layman's Bible Study Series

Forgiveness: Transforming You

Jim Melanson

Forgiveness: Transforming You

The Layman's Bible Study Series

© 2017 by James Melanson

All rights reserved. No part of this publication may be reproduced, stored in a retrieval system, or transmitted by any means – electronic, mechanical, photographic (photocopying), recording, or otherwise – without prior permission in writing from the author.

Printed by CreateSpace

ISBN: 978-0-9949203-8-6

More titles available at:
www.jimmelanson.ca

Editorial service provided by Dorathy Gass
www.metwritingservices.com

Cover Illustration licensed from iStockPhoto.com

Scripture is taken from THE HOLY BIBLE, NEW INTERNATIONAL VERSION®, NIV® Copyright © 1973, 1978, 1984, 2011 by Biblica, Inc.® Used by permission. All rights reserved worldwide.

This eBook may be given away to other people but may not be re-sold. This eBook may be quoted as you wish, but please reference the work:

Melanson, J. (2017). *Forgiveness: Transforming You.* The Layman's Perspective Series. Cobourg, ON: Melanson Publishing. www.jimmelanson.ca

Dedication

For my friend, Roxanne.

Chapter 1
The "F" Word

Forgiveness: there, I said it — the "F" word. It's a word that is often bandied about, frequently lied about, and for a lot of people, it comes without any instruction manual — not even a *cheat sheet*. You would think that if God wanted us to be so forgiving, He would have better equipped us to do so. Well, actually, He did. The instructions for forgiveness come to you when you understand more than society's perception of that single word. As with much of the Bible, focussing on the narrow aspects of text causes you to lose the full meaning and richness of the text you are focussing on.

There have been two recurring themes in my life: patience and forgiveness. That is to say, the Good Lord has provided me with a splendid number of opportunities to practice both virtues. Over the years, I've come to a new appreciation for, and approach to, forgiveness. Patience — well, I'm still working on that one, especially during rush hour.

"Forgiveness can't change the past, but it can change the future."[1]

I feel compelled to write about forgiveness because of my vast experience with it; that is, my vast experience with God forgiving me. Because of His enduring love, His incredible patience, and His infinite capacity to forgive, I have had to ask myself many times: how can I be anything *but* forgiving, to each and every person that I have felt wronged by? There is nothing that anyone has done to me that compares with the things that God has forgiven me for.

While I will be sharing a bit about myself, this book isn't about me. This book is about two things: helping you come closer to God, and helping you learn how to be truly forgiving.

There are many passages in the Bible that deal with forgiveness. My personal favourite is from the Gospel of Matthew, 18:21-35. It's called the *Parable of Ten Thousand Talents*; you may know it as the *Parable of the Unmerciful Servant*. This passage has been a guiding principal in my life for many years. It has helped me become a forgiving person, versus the person I used to be. I feel so strongly about this that I had the word "Ten Thousand" tattooed on my forearm where I could see it every day, all the time.

As I work at enriching my relationship with God, and strive to lead a life that is more in line with God's word and Jesus' teachings, forgiveness is something that I will always be mindful of and pursue at every opportunity. While there are many passages in the Bible about the topic, there isn't a lot of instruction on the topic. At least, that's what I thought. Once you study enough of the Bible, the path to forgiveness starts to be revealed.

I'm also going to go beyond the Bible. I'm going to talk about real-world examples of forgiveness, as well as anger, fear, empathy, self-understanding, cognitive bias, and looking at events with a different perspective. Understanding the psychology of fear and anger are a valuable component of forgiveness. I'm going to provide some very *practical* advice, not just biblical advice, on things that you can ruminate upon in your growing understanding of forgiveness.

At the end of the book, you'll still be the same person you are now. Mastering forgiveness doesn't come overnight, but it does come. With your own desire and diligence, you can transform yourself from an anxiety-ridden, hateful, always disappointed person, to someone who smiles, is calm, and lets a lot of things roll off their back. You will learn to shortcut your path to forgiveness for things that would have previously sent you into a tailspin for hours, days, or weeks.

Ultimately, forgiveness for yourself and for others comes from one place: God's love. We'll explore this through the powerful words of Jesus Christ as well as the examples set by our Saviour and so many others in the Bible. Being able to forgive and let go of fear will enrich your enjoyment of life and have a positive effect on your relationships. Forgiveness can be a powerful change in the world and in your own life. It will transform you in ways that you may have, until now, only longed for.

The absence of forgiveness isn't about the Unforgiven; it's about those who are unforgiving.

Chapter 2

What is forgiveness?

"But they're going to get away with it?"

"Aren't they going to get punished?"

"They hurt me, bad; they need to suffer as well."

"I'm not going to let them get away with this; I want to hurt them too."

"They need to pay for what they did to me."

Have you ever said any of those things or things like that? Those aren't very forgiving statements, are they? What else is missing from those statements?

There are lots of things missing from them: love, compassion, understanding, ability to see through another's eyes, arrogance, pride, perhaps even some narcissism. So, this brings us to the first question we have to ask in our pursuit: what is forgiveness? How do we define it?

As a child, I was taught that when you do something wrong, you say, "I'm sorry." On the other side of that, I was taught that when someone says, "I'm sorry," then the correct response is, "that's okay." I think we all understand that this is an appropriate exemplar for a child, but unfortunately, our training in the art of forgiveness doesn't really progress beyond that. Many of us are left floundering at times in a riptide of emotions to figure out what forgiveness is: how do you forgive, are we actually forgiving, or just mouthing the words, or can we be truly forgiven?

With this book, I want to help you find *your* path to being a forgiving person. Having been someone that was a bitter, hate-filled, unrepentant, anxiety-ridden person, I'm going to be writing in part from my own experience. My life is now absent of all those things. I want to share that overwhelming feeling of peace and calm with you.

> "Forgiveness is not an occasional act, it is a constant attitude." - Martin Luther King Jr.

The first step, however, is to figure out exactly what it is that forgiveness means. When I turned to the Bible in pursuit of the art of forgiveness, I realised that forgiveness wasn't something that you did: forgiveness comes from who you are. So, my first step was to realise that I was not in pursuit of the *art of forgiveness*, rather, I was in pursuit of a *forgiving nature* (dispositional forgiveness). Perhaps it would be more accurate to say that I was in pursuit of the personal transformation that would have my inherent nature become forgiving, rather than have to generate forgiveness.

Merriam-Webster defines *forgive* as a transitive verb with the meanings:

> 1a) To give up resentment of or claim to requital (something given in return, compensation, or retaliation), e.g. *forgive* an insult.

> 1b) To grant relief from payment of, e.g. *forgive* a debt.

2) To cease to feel resentment against (an offender), e.g. *forgive* one's enemies.

As a transitive verb, the word "forgive" always takes a direct object. That means you forgive someone. To put that another way, when you forgive, there is something specific that you are being forgiving about.

> "Forgiveness allows us to let go of the pain in the memory, and if we let go of the pain in the memory we can have the memory but it does not control us. When memory controls us we are then the puppets of the past." - Alexandra Asseily: founder of the Centre for Lebanese Studies at St. Antony's College (Oxford University)

Some may say, tongue-in-cheek, that forgiveness is, "giving up my right to hurt you, for hurting me."[2] While this may seem like a glib statement, it does contain an accurate description. It is saying that by forgiving you are giving up a claim of *requital*. When we are new to the concept of pursuing the state of forgiveness for those who have wronged us, one of the things that we are trying to get away from is retaliation.

> "An eye for an eye only ends up making the whole world blind." - Mahatma Gandhi

While it may be odd to quote a lawyer in a book about forgiveness, Marelisa Fabrega offers the following re-definition of forgiveness in an article she wrote:[3]

- Forgiveness is about freeing up and putting to better use the energy that is being consumed by holding on to grudges, harboring resentments, and nursing old wounds.
- Forgiveness is about moving on.
- Forgiveness is about choosing serenity and happiness over righteous anger.
- Forgiveness is about refusing to replay past hurts in your mind over and over again, like a broken record.
- Forgiveness is about realizing that anger and resentment don't serve you well.
- Forgiveness is about giving yourself a clean slate.

We have been raised to understand that forgiveness is something that you can offer, that you can withhold, that you can seek, or that you can ignore. However, that's not entirely accurate. While the act of forgiving requires something to be forgiven, a forgiving nature comes from who you are. It's a reflection of who you intrinsically are — that part of you which is shaped by the Christ principle whether you are a believer, an unbeliever, an apostate, or an atheist.

Based on the idea of the "Christophic principle",[4] the Christ principle is what I call the way of life that Jesus wants mankind to emulate: brotherly love, kindness, compassion, forgiveness, humility, gentleness, etc. These are all things that need to come from our nature; to come from inside of us naturally. Yes, we can pay lip-service to them, we can "fake it till we make it", but if it isn't truly who we are, then it benefits us nothing. In fact, the "fake it till we make it" approach will only harm you. It fools you because you see yourself, reflected in others, doing the right thing. The damage comes because you haven't truly settled those parts of your nature that will allow you to become that person. I'm speaking from my own experience, and careful observation of those I have shared my life with. It's a journey, an uphill one at times, but it's one of the most important journeys you will ever make.

The Holy Bible tells us frequently of the need to be forgiving, and why we need to be forgiving. There are scant few passages that tell us *how* to be forgiving. This is because forgiveness inherently comes from love: love for our fellow man, love for ourselves, and love for God.

In Leviticus 19:9-18 we read instructions on how we should love our fellow man. In Matthew 22:39 and Mark 12:31 we read the command to *"Love your neighbour as yourself."* This may raise a question regarding some other Old Testament passages that call for, *"eye for eye, tooth for tooth"* (Exodus 21:23-25, Leviticus 24:19-20). You need to remember that the old covenant law (Mosaic Law) does not apply to Christians (Acts 15:5-29).

At the Sermon on the Mount, Jesus reiterated Leviticus 19:18 when he said:

> *"You have heard that it was said, 'Love your neighbor and hate your enemy.' But I tell you, love your enemies and pray for those who persecute you, that you may be children of your Father in heaven. He causes his sun to rise on the evil and the good, and sends rain on the righteous and the unrighteous. If you love those who love you, what reward will you get? Are not even the tax collectors doing that? And if you greet only your own people, what are you doing more than others? Do not even pagans do that? Be perfect, therefore, as your heavenly Father is perfect." (Matthew 5:43-48)*

Love is the catalyst for change in our life. It is definitely the catalyst for forgiveness. But this still leaves us with the question, "what does forgiveness look like on a day to day basis?" Most of us have a lifetime of unlearning to do when it comes to the "F" word. So, my first step was to look for the best example of what forgiveness is in the Bible. I found it in Paul's letter to the church at Ephesus:

> *"Let all bitterness and wrath and anger and clamour and slander be put away from you, along with all malice. And be kind to one another, tender-hearted, forgiving each other, just as God in Christ also has forgiven you." (Ephesians 4:31-32)*

For me, that's a good answer to the question, biblically speaking. However, we need to expand on that definition of forgiveness and gain a deeper understanding of it.

In a Bible study series about forgiveness, Rev. Wilson of Greenville Presbyterian Theological Seminary explains the above two verses this way:[5]

> "In this passage, Paul uses a word for forgiveness that includes the idea of "giving graciously" or giving something which isn't deserved. So, God is commanding us to forgive others in a tender-hearted way (even when that forgiveness isn't deserved) "just as God in Christ also has forgiven" us. This is probably the most important text for explaining forgiveness! Here, God is clearly aligning our forgiveness with His. God offers forgiveness of sin to all men everywhere who repent and put their faith in Jesus Christ (Acts 2:38, 3:18-21, 17:30-31). There are two parts to God's forgiveness: (1) the attitude and offer of forgiveness through the Gospel, which is preached to all nations; and (2) the gracious forgiveness of all those who actually repent and believe in Christ for salvation.

> Likewise, our forgiveness is defined by those same two elements. First, we are to be tender-hearted in attitude – willing to forgive all those who offend or sin against us. Second, we are to actually forgive those who repent and come asking for forgiveness."

I found a very inspiring checklist of what forgiveness looks like in an article posted on the Christian Courier website, written by author and teacher R. Wayne Jackson:[6]

> Our forgiveness of each other has to do more with an attitude than a specific act. Reflect upon the following principles which highlight the sort of temperament that one must cultivate if he would be Christ-like (Luke 23:34).
>
> - The forgiving person does not attempt to take revenge upon those who have wronged him (Romans 12:17).
>
> - The forgiving person does not hate the offender; rather, in spite of the person's evil, he loves (agape) him still. For the meaning of agape love, see our article, "The Challenge of Agape Love."
>
> - The forgiving person is kindly disposed and tenderhearted *(sic)* toward his adversary (Ephesians 4:32).
>
> - The forgiving person is approachable; he leaves the door for reconciliation wide open and longs for the welfare of the transgressor.
>
> - The forgiving person is not merely passive in waiting for the offender to repent; he actively seeks

the repentance of the one who wronged him (Matthew 18:15-17).

While I like Wayne Jackson's elucidation on the topic, I think that the best working explanation of forgiveness comes from the Puritan preacher Thomas Watson through a sermon by John Piper:[7]

> Let me begin with a definition of forgiveness that we owe to each other. It comes from Thomas Watson about 300 years ago. He is commenting on the Lord's Prayer, "Forgive us our debts as we forgive our debtors," and asks,
>
> Question: When do we forgive others?
>
> Answer: When we strive against all thoughts of revenge; when we will not do our enemies' mischief, but wish well to them, grieve at their calamities, pray for them, seek reconciliation with them, and show ourselves ready on all occasions to relieve them. (Thomas Watson, Body of Divinity, p. 581)
>
> I think this is a very biblical definition of forgiveness. Each of its parts comes from a passage of Scripture.
>
> 1. Resist thoughts of revenge: Romans 12:19, "Never take your own revenge, beloved, but leave room for the wrath of God, for it is written, 'Vengeance is Mine, I will repay,' says the Lord."
>
> 2. Don't seek to do them mischief: 1 Thessalonians 5:15, "See that no one repays another with evil for evil.
>
> 3. Wish well to them: Luke 6:28, "Bless those who curse you."

4. Grieve at their calamities: Proverbs 24:17, "Do not rejoice when your enemy falls, and do not let your heart be glad when he stumbles."

5. Pray for them: Matthew 5:44, "But I say to you, love your enemies, and pray for those who persecute you."

6. Seek reconciliation with them: Romans 12:18, "If possible, so far as it depends on you, be at peace with all men."

7. Be always willing to come to their relief: Exodus 23:4, "If you meet your enemy's ox or his donkey wandering away, you shall surely return it to him."

Here is forgiveness: when you feel that someone is your enemy or when you simply feel that you or someone you care about has been wronged, forgiveness means,

1. resisting revenge,

2. not returning evil for evil,

3. wishing them well,

4. grieving at their calamities,

5. praying for their welfare,

6. seeking reconciliation so far as it depends on you,

7. and coming to their aid in distress.

Both John Piper and Wayne Jackson have provided very clear and understandable definitions that are aligned with Paul's epistle; they are biblically sound.

At the start of the chapter, I quoted a few things you may have heard, or even said, over the years. When I asked what was missing from those statements, the first item I listed was "love".

Dallas Willard wrote:[8]

> "We do well to note, however, that *love* is the foundation of the spiritual life and *joy* is a key component in the Christ life. Joy is not pleasure, a mere sensation, but a pervasive and constant sense of well-being."

For myself, I've found that simple fact to be crucial in my understanding of forgiveness, and my pursuit of that state in my life. When a heart has no love in it, it has no forgiveness; but a heart that is filled with love for God is also filled with the capacity to forgive. A heart that is filled with God's love has no room for competing emotions.

As we move on through this book, you need to come to an understanding of what forgiveness means for you. Right now, you have your own experiential understanding of forgiveness, be it giving or receiving. As we explore this topic together, I also hope that you will define a goal for the forgiving person that you want to *become*: having a limitless capacity for forgiveness and love that is based on the example of Jesus Christ and your love for God.

Chapter 3

What Forgiveness is *Not*

Unfortunately, there is a great deal of misunderstanding about what a truly forgiving nature means. We are humans, we are fallible, and in our efforts to pursue a higher level of understanding we can make some mistakes along the way. The effect of this is that we can make things more difficult for ourselves by trying to anthropomorphize God's intentions into human terms. One way we do this is through a literal application of what is intended to be concepts and understanding. To a case in point, many people make the mistaken belief that forgiveness means forgetting.

To put it succinctly, Toussaint et al. wrote in the Journal of Behavioral Medicine:[9]

> "Importantly, forgiveness is not condoning, excusing, denying, minimizing, or forgetting the wrong."

Forgiveness is not forgetting

This is a mistake made when people are exploring their capacity for forgiveness. As Dr. Sam Storms, American Calvinist author and pastor wrote:[10]

> "Forgive and forget," we have been told by so many through the years. It's a nice saying, but highly misleading. Why?
>
> First of all, God does not forget, notwithstanding what you think Jeremiah 31:34 is saying ("For I will forgive their

iniquity, and I will remember their sin no more"). This language of the prophet is metaphor, a word picture, designed to emphasize God's gracious determination and resolve not to hold us liable for our sin. He has canceled the debt and will never demand payment. If God could literally "forget" it would undermine the truth of his omniscience. God always has and always will know all things, but he has promised never to use our sin against us or treat us as if the reality of our sin were present in his mind.

Second, "forgive and forget", quite simply, is psychologically impossible. As soon as you make up your mind to forget something you can be assured that, in most instances, it is the one thing that will linger at the forefront of your conscious thinking. We all forget things, but we do it unintentionally over the course of time. Life and experience and old age work to erase certain things from our memory, but that is rarely if ever the case with sins committed against us and the wounds we have suffered.

Third, to think that forgiving demands forgetting can be emotionally devastating. Let's suppose that Jane succeeds for two months in forgetting Sally's betrayal of her. She's getting along well and hasn't given a second thought to Sally's sin. Then Jane is told that Sally did the same thing to Mary and she immediately remembers the offense she herself endured. She is suddenly riddled with guilt for having failed to forget. What she thought she had forever put out of her mind now comes rushing back involuntarily and she feels like an utter failure for not having "truly" forgiven her friend. Worse still, she now feels like a hypocrite for having promised to forget only to once again feel anger and resentment toward Sally. Not only is Jane emotionally devastated, she now realizes how impossible it is to literally forget something so painful. This makes her extremely reluctant ever to forgive anyone again, knowing in her heart that she is incapable of forgetting.

As Dr. Storm said, it's impossible to forget being wronged. I've known this for a long time, as I'm sure you do. Lack of ability to forget should not be a determining factor on whether you are going to have forgiveness.

The phrase "forgive and forget" is, like the passage in Jeremiah, a metaphor. The forget part simply means that when we forgive, we no longer hold on to the hurt, or rather, the hurt no longer holds on to us. While time itself will cause me to forget many things, that is, remove them from my conscious memory, we never truly forget anything. Everything we have done, read, heard, or said is locked away in our brain.[11,12,13,14]

Have you ever tried to tell a joke, but as you are telling the joke you suddenly remember the original text and that you are telling it wrong? Have you ever had to explain your actions to the boss, and then as you are giving the explanation, you realise you're wrong about the facts because they resurface? We'll be exploring the connection between verbalization and memory later on, but these simple examples show you that memories are there and they are present in more detail than you think.

The point I'm making is that "forgive and forget" has meaning, but not the meaning people attribute to it. You will never *forget*, but you can *move past* something and relegate it to your subconscious.

> "Forgiveness is about empowering yourself, rather than empowering your past." - T.D. Jakes

Forgiveness does not mean you don't hurt

We are emotional creatures, we feel fear and love. Sometimes we encounter betrayal, attacks, mean-spirited actions, and loss at the hands of others. To deny the fact that we feel in reaction to these things would be denying the very essence of the image in which God created us - His image.

> "Walking around with a painted-on smile when you are emotionally dying inside is not forgiveness. In scripture we never see Jesus pretend. When he is sad, he cries (John 11:35). When he is angry, he turns over the tables in the temple (John 2:15-16). When he is lonely, he cries to his Daddy (Matthew 26:39). Christianity is not about denying a wound caused by another. Someone has betrayed your trust, damaged your soul, or caused a loss. You are justified in recognizing the hurt instigated by another's sinful or poor choices."[15]

To not hurt would make us less human; it would mean that we were dead inside and incapable of feeling. God wants us to enjoy the life He has given us (Jeremiah 29:11, John 10:10, 1 Timothy 6:17). However, the ability to feel joy means that we have the ability to feel, which means we can feel pain as well. It is, poetically speaking, one of the joys embedded within the mystery of life.

Hurt, however, can heal. It can be assuaged through understanding, time and distance, perspective, and ultimately it can be healed through the power of God's love for you. When you immerse yourself in His love, healing will flow. Yes, I know that's a very touchy-feely and non-specific statement, but that doesn't make it any less true. In fact, biblically speaking, God acknowledges that healing is a process:

> *"In your anger do not sin": Do not let the sun go down while you are still angry, and do not give the devil a foothold. (Ephesians 4:26-27)*

Again, the misunderstanding of forgiveness, of the process, can lead us to think we are unable to be forgiving or not pursue forgiveness. While I do contend that forgiveness is a *state of being*, that does not mean it occurs instantaneously. Being forgiving is the nature we strive for. As humans, however, we have complex psychological and emotional bodies that need to process life and our response to our experiences. We need to process that experience, we need to examine ourselves and relevant perspectives, and we need time to heal.

In the above verse from Ephesians, verse 27 is an exhortation to us not to let the healing process and our reach for forgiveness take too long. The worry is that the longer you are in a state that lacks forgiveness, the easier it is for the Devil to be at work: sowing discord between us, bringing forth hateful words from us, taking revenge out of frustration, etc.

God is there for us. If we reach out to Him in prayer, He will aid us in our healing. Don't underestimate the power of prayer for our own needs. Seek His healing and His peace; through these, the rest of the psychological and emotional process of moving from hurt/grief to healing and forgiveness will be made much easier.

> *Rejoice in the Lord always. I will say it again: Rejoice! Let your gentleness be evident to all. The Lord is near. Do not be anxious about anything, but in every situation, by prayer and petition, with thanksgiving, present your requests to God. And the peace of God, which transcends all understanding, will guard your hearts and your minds in Christ Jesus. (Philippians 4:4-7)*

In chapter nine I will discuss changing your perspective; suffice it to say for now that part of this process of healing from the hurt involves understanding the offender and understanding ourselves. The way forward from hurt is to grow as a person; one of the most important paths in this regard is the path of your spiritual formation. In Matthew 13 (The Parable of the Sower), when asked why He spoke in parables, part of Jesus' answer was:

> *"Listen then to what the parable of the sower means: When anyone hears the message about the kingdom and does not understand it, the evil one comes and snatches away what was sown in their heart. This is the seed sown along the path. The seed falling on rocky ground refers to someone who hears the word and at once receives it with joy. But since they have no root, they last only a short time. When trouble or persecution comes because of the word, they quickly fall away. The seed falling among the thorns refers to someone who hears the word, but the worries of this life and the deceitfulness of wealth choke the word, making it unfruitful. But the seed falling on good soil refers to someone who hears the word and understands it. This is the one who produces a crop, yielding a hundred, sixty or thirty times what was sown."*

So, what does this have to do with hurting? As we grow and mature in our spiritual formation, as we strengthen and deepen our relationship with God, we open our eyes to new understanding. As we grow in this way, God works to help us heal our hurts and wounds.

> *"He heals the broken hearted and binds up their wounds."*
> *(Psalm 147:3)*

Pastor Mark Altrogge, senior pastor at Saving Grace Church, wrote:[16]

> "When we are sinned against, it can be devastating, life-shattering, disillusioning, disorienting. Some sins are easy to forgive, but others can take a long time, much prayer, and much help from God. When someone's reeling in pain, the first thing they need is our compassion and sympathy, not a quick encouragement to forgive. That will probably be part of the process of helping someone, but not the first step. I regret that at times in the past I was incredibly insensitive to some people's pain and way too quick to suggest that they meet with those who'd sinned against them and grant forgiveness."

Pursuing that *state of forgiveness*, our desired nature to be forgiving, is vital to our own health and happiness. However, pursuing it in a psychologically and emotionally safe way is also important. God is there to support us and help us with this. Rely on Him for strength, courage, and insight, but do not fail to gently work your way through the process of healing.

"To forgive is to set a prisoner free and discover that the prisoner was you." - Lewis B. Smedes

Forgiveness doesn't mean you have to let them hurt you again

When we forgive and put away our need for retribution, retaliation, requital, etc.; this does not mean that we have to expose our self to more hurt from that person. It does not mean that we must repeatedly place our emotions in the path of someone's steamroller of mental/emotional/physical assault. Being a forgiving person does not mean we are a doormat or a football for other people's emotions.

So how does one be forgiving and yet protect themselves from future hurt? For myself, I have found the response to this is that just because I have been forgiving, does not mean I need to keep a person in my life. There have been several people whom I chose to stop associating with because they proved untrustworthy even after forgiveness. I'll still speak with them; if they ask me for assistance I'll still give it; however, I don't interact with them socially or emotionally. I set healthy and positive boundaries.

Yes, you will find forgiven people trying to manipulate you. They may say something like, "If you've forgiven me, you wouldn't be shutting me out" or "if you don't trust me then you haven't really forgiven me" or "you're not much of a Christian if you can't forgive me." Unfortunately, the people who say these things to manipulate you don't understand forgiveness, and they are reacting out of anger (fear) that you aren't going to let them close enough (to hurt you again).

My response is that I just choose not to be close to them anymore. There is nothing about forgiveness that requires we be a doormat, a punching bag, or a repeated victim. Being forgiving does not mean that you need to continue to be manipulated by others.

Remember that forgiveness and trust are not the same things. Just because your nature is to forgive them and put the past behind you, does not mean you automatically begin trusting them again. Quoting Pastor Mark Altrogge again:[16]

> "Forgiveness is instantaneous; trust is earned over time. If a drunkard comes to church and turns to Christ, God forgives him immediately, but he shouldn't become a leader the next day. If someone asks our forgiveness for hurting us, we can

> forgive them, but it doesn't necessarily mean they've changed. It's not wrong to want to see a track record of change before trusting someone again, even if we've forgiven them."

In a *RELEVANT Magazine* article, writer and speaker Todd Morrison made two points about forgiveness and reconciliation, highlighting that it is not necessarily part of forgiveness:[17]

> "Most of us need very little time to recall the petty conflicts we've had with close friends. Petty conflicts can tear relationships apart for a lifetime unless forgiveness and reconciliation are pursued and realized."

Then further down in the article:

> "Having said that, there are relationships that have become so toxic and unhealthy that they cannot be reconciled. There are people who have wounded us to such a degree that it is not healthy for us to be in relationship with them. These are the people with whom we need to establish boundaries that create a safe buffer between our world and theirs. Yet, for the sake of our own spiritual and emotional health, it is critical that we forgive these people—even when relational reconciliation is not our goal."

Being forgiving does not mean there is no justice

I've found the simplest illustration to the question of whether forgiveness does not mean justice is pursued, in the question to Jesus about paying the imperial tax to Caesar. A group of Pharisees tried to trap Jesus by asking Him if people should pay their taxes to Caesar, because if Jesus said that they should not, then He would be arrested. Instead, His response was:

> *... Then he said to them, "So give back to Caesar what is Caesar's, and to God what is God's." (Matthew 22:21)*

Revenge and justice are principally the same thing, but from different perspectives. Revenge is a personal response to injustice, whereas justice is a socially defined legal response. Unfortunately, there is often little socially-defined legal responses to many actions that hurt us: infidelity, insults, betrayal, backstabbing, etc.

This is where we must understand that avenging wrongs done to us is the purview of God:

> *Do not take revenge, my dear friends, but leave room for God's wrath, for it is written: "It is mine to avenge; I will repay," says the Lord. (Romans 12:19)*

While the above verse is fairly well known, it's important to put it in context. In Romans 12, the letter to Rome is telling us how we should strive to live our lives: sacrifice, humble service, and love in action. Verses 17-18 of that chapter add an extra dimension to verse 19:

> *Do not repay anyone evil for evil. Be careful to do what is right in the eyes of everyone. If it is possible, as far as it depends on you, live at peace with everyone.*

What this is telling us is that we should not be pursuing justice or requital for ourselves. In that, is an inherent trap that many people fall into, as I have myself. We tell our self that we are simply pursuing justice when in fact, we are pursuing revenge through justice. If you need to keep telling yourself you are just pursuing justice, then you really need to take a closer look at your motivations. A good test for this is imagining the outcome of that pursuit of justice. If that person is found guilty and punished, will you rejoice? If so, then you seriously need to get on your knees and start praying — *for yourself.* If you are forgiving, then you will not take joy in the misfortune of the other person, even if it is warranted and just, according to the terms of man.

The phrase "terms of man" is an important point. The pursuit of justice comes from the legal system of our society, and we must honour that (1 Peter 2:13-17, Romans 13:1-7). We have laws to define how society needs to coexist together. These laws make our lives orderly, right, and ultimately, safe. Because we forgive the person for their actions does not abrogate that person's obligation to answer to society. Forgiveness also does not remove our need to participate in that justice system, in the manner that we are required to participate in it. We may be required to participate as a witness or as a jury member.

The important distinction here is that forgiving someone for a criminal act does not mean there will not be justice here on earth. Legal justice is pursued in accordance with the laws of man — for the good of the community. You must not pursue justice, however, for your own personal hurt, as this is the justice that belongs in the hands of God (*"… and to God what is God's."*).

I know there are Christians that have a problem with the idea of serving on a jury, for biblical reasons: we are not supposed to judge others (Matthew 7:1). Unfortunately, as with many other passages, they interpret this verse alone and without context. If you read the whole chapter of Matthew 7, you will see that Jesus is telling us not to be *judgemental*, but that we are to be *discerning*.

In Matthew 7:6, He says, *"Do not give to the dogs what is sacred; do not throw your pearls to the pigs."* To decide whether a person is a dog or a pig, you need to use discernment. In verse 15, He warns us to, *"Watch out for false prophets."* We can only determine who is a false prophet, for our own benefit, by using discernment. In John 7:24, at the Festival of Tabernacles, speaking to the crowd, a crowd who accused Jesus of being demon-possessed, He told them, *"Stop judging by mere appearances, but instead judge correctly."* Again, He was instructing them to use discernment.

When we are asked to serve on a jury, we are being asked to apply discernment, not judgement. Has the prosecution made their case? Have they proven the facts? Has the defence created reasonable doubt? These are not about judging the person; these questions are about your discernment of the facts. There can indeed be justice, with forgiveness.

Clinical psychologist Dr. Raymond Richmond wrote:[18]

> "In contrast to all this human illusion—and folly—you have another option. That is, when you are hurt, you don't have to fight back, trying to hurt others as they have hurt you. If you trust in God's perfect justice to protect you, you can accept all injury quietly, peacefully, and without grumbling or protest. Despite your injuries, you can give patience, understanding, compassion, forbearance, mercy, and forgiveness to those who hurt you, all the while praying that they will repent their wickedness."

"You're not letting people off the hook, you are letting go of the resentment that is destroying you." - Corine Gatti

Forgiveness does not mean you are unimportant or weak

If you have read and paid attention to the New Testament, as well as the Old, it should be obvious how important you are to

God. But with that importance, comes humbleness. Again, we find a confusing idea: how can one be so important, yet also need to be so humble?

In his book, *What on Earth Am I Here For? The Purpose Driven Life* evangelical Christian author and pastor, Rick Warren, wrote the following:[19]

> "True humility is not thinking less of yourself; it is thinking of yourself less."

What this is saying is that having humility does not mean you believe you are unworthy or worthless. Humility, putting others first, is a choice that we make and I can tell you from personal experience, that this is an expression of strength.

> "... the weak can never forgive. Forgiveness is an attribute of the strong." - Mahatma Gandhi

The second law of thermodynamics concerns entropy, which is about the gradual decline into disorder for a system's thermal energy. I submit that this effect is also prevalent in the condition of human thought and emotion. When we remove love, happiness, joy, etc. from our lives, they are replaced by disorder (fear, anxiety, anger, etc.). However, when we work to fill ourselves with love, happiness, and joy, we remove the amount of available space those negatives have in our psyche. The key word there is "work".

Being angry, while not enjoyable, is easy; hating someone is easy; feeling victimised is easy; letting loose with spiteful words is easy. Conversely, when we work to have a forgiving nature, we are making an effort. When we take the time to work through hurt so that we can get to the place that God wants us to be, we must make an effort. When we put hurtful actions aside and continue to treat the offender with kindness, we must make an effort to do that, an effort that is sometimes Herculean.

In an article titled "Is Forgiveness a Sign of Weakness in Leaders?" journalist Sandy Clarke writes:[20]

> "Sometimes, forgiveness is seen as a weakness, chosen by those who lack the stomach for confrontation and so give up an opportunity for justice. But, in truth, forgiveness is a strength, which is why so many struggle to fully embrace it.
>
> The weakness lies in our ego, in our need to be appeased and acknowledged as someone who has been wronged, in a way that suggests that we believe life should never run against our expectations.
>
> Holding onto grudges and past ills that can't be changed is a waste of energy that could be better put to use moving ourselves and our ambitions forward. Forgiveness, therefore, is more than a strength—it's the smart move to make. Otherwise, the painful past remains in your head, rent-free, taking up a large space where positive emotions could be working to inspire and motivate."

Charles Spurgeon, whom I love to read and quote, put forward this goal for us to work towards in pursuit of a forgiving nature:[21]

> "Remember, when you have conquered yourself you have conquered the world. You have overcome everybody when you have so fully overcome your own spirit that you remain content with that which naturally would excite your wrath."

Being forgiving is a demonstration of commitment, courage, and strength. When you forgive you are demonstrating your faith in

God; you are expressing the love that He fills you with; you are an agent of change for the betterment of the world through the example you set for others to follow. None of these things is the purview of the weak; they are in the domain of strength and courage.

> "Forgiveness is not a feeling - it's a decision we make because we want to do what's right before God. It's a quality decision that won't be easy and it may take time to get through the process, depending on the severity of the offense." - Joyce Meyer

Summary

We pay lip service to forgiveness (self-righteous forgiveness) when we want to appear to be right, appear to be good, even if we are doing it to appear that way just to ourselves (pride). True forgiveness, however, comes from a place of love; a pervading love that fills our lives. Such a powerful, transformative, and all-encompassing love can only come from God through the power of the Holy Spirit residing in you. You can only have the true effect of that power when you work to empty yourself of the negative and fill that void with what comes from Him. This means you must work at it.

Being forgiving does not mean that another's offence is right, okay, or without consequences. It does not mean that there is no justice. *Why* justice is pursued is what's important. Don't fool yourself into thinking you are being forgiving while pursuing justice if there is any glee or happiness in your heart at the other person's punishment, as that is not truly forgiveness. Instead, let justice pursue itself and contribute to it only as required. God takes no joy in your failures, nor should you take joy in another's.

Being forgiving is not caused by a lack of strength or courage; true forgiveness can only come from strength. It comes from the strength of your commitment to transforming yourself into a follower of the Christ principle, and therefore, someone filled with God's love. It comes from your courage to stand up for what is right, rather than allow yourself to descend with the entropy of anger and hatred. The upside of so much work is the life of joy, peace, love, *and forgiveness* that the Holy Spirit will fill us with through all of our days.

Chapter 4

Why We Need to Forgive

In his book *The Weight of Glory*, C.S. Lewis puts daily forgiveness into perspective for us:[22]

> "This is hard. It is perhaps not so hard to forgive a single great injury. But to forgive the incessant provocations of daily life—to keep on forgiving the bossy mother-in-law, the bullying husband, the nagging wife, the selfish daughter, the deceitful son—how can we do it? Only, I think, by remembering where we stand, by meaning our words when we say in our prayers each night 'forgive our trespasses as we forgive those that trespass against us.' We are offered forgiveness on no other terms. To refuse it is to refuse God's mercy for ourselves. There is no hint of exceptions and God means what He says."

In her book *Do Yourself a Favor ... Forgive*, Bible teacher and author Joyce Meyer calls unforgiveness a poison. She says:[23]

> "Many people ruin their health and their lives by taking the poison of bitterness, resentment and unforgiveness."

She goes on to put it quite succinctly:

> "Unforgiveness is spiritual filthiness, so get washed in the water of God's Word to forgive and stay clean."

Some people enjoy anger; they get caught up in the self-righteous indignation because it's one of the few things in life that give them a sense of power. Some people prefer to wear the offence against them like a badge of honour. The commiseration and expressions of shock from their friends and family actually provide an attachment or connection to others that may have been absent or diminished in their lives. The people who hold on to that anger, resentment, and hurt without letting it go through forgiveness, are putting themselves ahead of God's will. Additionally, from a mundane perspective, they are damaging relationships rather than healing them; they are damaging their own health; they are damaging their community of family and friends.

When we refuse to forgive, we join the negative hate-cycle:[23]

> "Fear, anger, hate, and revenge are the most destructive forms of energy that a person can experience. These emotions can dominate your thinking and can lead you to commit negative acts. And if you commit a negative act, you in turn will become part of that negative cycle. What goes around comes around, no matter who you are. We see this time and time again in the news. By giving in to your fear, anger, and hate, you ultimately will be no different from those who wronged you in the first place."

In talking about forgiveness, it is clearly evident that we need to strive for a forgiving nature in answering the call of our Lord. To further our understanding of why we need to be forgiving, we must look at the two types of forgiveness: conditional and unconditional.

Conditional forgiveness takes place after the offender has asked for forgiveness, or made amends. Conditional forgiveness has an earthly requirement, which is not a divine requirement. God wants our forgiveness to be from love; he wants it to come from inside us, not for it to be based upon others. If we attach a requirement to the forgiveness we have, then are we truly being forgiving?

Quoting Toussaint (et al.) again:[9]

> "This study found that conditional forgiveness of others was associated with increased mortality risk. Apologies, amends, and assurances certainly facilitate the forgiveness process (Allan et al.,2006; Exline et al.,2003), but if these acts of contrition are viewed as necessary conditions or prerequisites required before forgiveness can be offered, then there will likely be fewer instances of forthcoming forgiveness for that individual. This is due simply to the fact that those who cause an offense will not always fulfill such conditions, regardless of their appropriateness, and the offended party does not have the power to make them occur. Conceptualizing these responses as requirements for forgiveness also prevents access to forgiveness for those who are unable to identify whether acts of contrition are occurring, for instance, in cases where the wrongdoer is deceased or no longer present for other reasons."

Unconditional forgiveness comes from our nature, from who we are, from our worldview and our spiritual view, and ultimately from God's love filling our life.

> "An unconditional perspective on forgiveness allows the process to begin whenever the offended party chooses, without the necessity of waiting for particular responses from others. Placing conditions on offering forgiveness to others adds barriers that can translate into extended duration of unforgiveness and/or decreased frequency of forgiveness, both of which may ultimately yield poorer health and greater mortality risk."[9]

Unconditional forgiveness does not require an apology, it does not need justice, and it does not demand acknowledgement.

Unconditional forgiveness exists in its own right, coming from within us regardless of the acknowledgement or regret of another person. Unconditional forgiveness will heal us emotionally, psychologically, and physically.

"I can have peace of mind only when I forgive rather than judge." - Dr. Gerald Jampolsky

The Perpetual Victim - Conditional Forgiveness

South African Archbishop Desmond Tutu explained it this way:[24]

> "If the victim could forgive only when the culprit confessed, then the victim would be locked into the culprit's whim, locked into victimhood, whatever her own attitude and intention. That would be palpably unjust."

When you are unable to forgive a person, you become locked into a cyclic relationship of hurt and betrayal. Without forgiveness, the hurtful actions of another colours and taints all future interactions you will have with that person and perhaps others.[25] Not only will that pain be something you remember, but it will also be something that you experience repeatedly. You become trapped by the will of another person.

> "Perhaps So-And-So hurt or wronged you or someone you love, and you firmly believe that So-And-So does not deserve your forgiveness. Maybe the hurt or injustice was so vile you think you could never forgive So-And-So. Maybe So-And-So ruined your life. In retaliation, you have

> locked So-And-So out of your life, so that person will never hurt you or wrong you again…
>
> In truth, you have locked yourself in the prison of unforgiveness while So-And-So moves on with life. Instead of hurting So-And-So, unforgiveness is hurting you emotionally, physically, and spiritually. The consequences of unforgiveness may be more self-destructive than you realize."[26]

When we are unforgiving in our nature, unable to let go of hurt and heal, we become slaves to those negative feelings. They hold us, continue to torment and torture us, while keeping us isolated from the joy and peace available to us from God.

> "If you are waiting until the feeling to forgive comes upon you, it's unlikely to occur. Forgiveness should be an act of obedience to God because we trust him and believe he has our best interest at heart. God knows that hanging on to revenge, anger, and rage can destroy us spiritually, emotionally and physically. Christ paid too much for his Beloved ones to have them a slave to anything, much less hatred. He wants his children free. And a person is never free when weighed down with the ball and chain of bitterness. When the cold shackles of revenge are tightly clasped around our wrists, it's impossible to lift our hands in praise to Him."[15]

Exploring the reasons why people won't forgive, Pastor Ron Barnes writes the following about the lack of understanding some people have around the effects of not forgiving:[27]

> "<u>They won't forgive because they don't understand the damage it does to their hearts.</u>

Most everyone who willingly holds onto a grudge does not realize the damage they are doing to themselves. Unforgiveness always leads to bitterness, and bitterness always leads to a hardened heart, one that cannot love or trust anyone. It affects our ability as parents, spouses, or even friends. Everyone can tell a bitter person; they're the ones who have become abusive, hard, quick-tempered, stubborn, unfriendly, and cold, the offense may be years gone and long forgotten by the other party, but the effects remain long after the fact. Saints, we must understand this: the only person unforgiveness hurts is the unforgiver!"

There are some people who enjoy being the victim, as it provides an excuse for their laziness about life. Is this you? Do you really want to be the victim all of your life? Is it time to change that? One of the keys of breaking the "I'm a victim, oh-woe-is-me" mindset is to start practising forgiveness. Once you take away the crutch of your blame, you will be compelled to move forward and start overcoming that destructive mental trait. Marelisa Febrega went on to say this in her previously cited article:[3]

> "In *Forgiveness: How to Make Peace With Your Past and Get on With Your Life'*, Sidney B. Simon and Suzanne Simon explain that for many people, not forgiving provides them with an excuse for everything that is wrong in their life.
>
> They use the fact that so-and-so did this-or-that to them to explain why they can't achieve certain life goals. If only that hadn't happened to them, then their life would be much better than it is. That is, they use the hurt that they experienced to get off the hook. If they forgive and heal, then they're out of an excuse.

> Stop telling yourself that because certain things happened to you in the past, you can't have what you want in the present or in the future. Instead, take responsibility for getting on with your life, in spite of anything that anyone may have done to you."

Sometimes the victim mentality is something that comes from events truly outside of your control. It can be easy to fall into that trap and allow it to control your definition of who you are, what life is for you, or how you see the world. Allowing the victimisation to continue well beyond the event itself will destroy only one person: *you.*

Sunny Jacobs and her husband were imprisoned for the murder of two policemen in Florida in 1976. After 17 years of incarceration, new evidence exonerated both her and her husband. However, her husband had already been executed for the murder, in a botched execution that required three jolts of electricity in the electric chair. During her incarceration, both of her parents were killed in a car crash. When she went to jail, she had two children, aged nine years and ten months. When Sunny was released, she was a widow, an orphan, and a grandmother. In the final outcome of her situation, it was shown that evidence had been falsified and witnesses had been tampered with, yet those who did this were never held accountable. This is what she had to say about forgiveness during an interview ten years after her release:[28]

> "If you're feeling sorry for yourself, it's hard to see past that *(self-righteous anger)* ... and the only way out of that is forgiveness, the only way out of it, there is no other way ... the next question is how long does it take? The rest of your life, that's how long that it takes; and how long is that? Every day."

TV and radio personality, Merri Dee, makes two important points in her book *Merri Dee, Life Lessons on Faith, Forgiveness & Grace*:[29]

> "Stuff happens: In your life, there are two events over which you have no control — the day you are born and the day you die. What's in between is yours to fill with gratitude or despair. I invite you to fill it with gratitude because it doesn't really matter what happens to you, what truly matters is how you respond to what happens. Some of those days will be heart-pounding moments. Deal with it, because stuff happens." (p. 162)

> "Forgive: Dump regrets! Whatever happened to you or by you is possibly over and done with. Forgive others and forgive yourself. Accept your mistakes, make amends and keep moving forward. I understand that forgiveness is not easy, but when it is achieved wholly, both people win. Holding onto bitterness and anger only hardens your heart and is like drinking poison while expecting the other person to die. It just won't happen." (p.163)

American President Bill Clinton counts Nelson Mandela as one of his friends. He once asked the man about his attitude toward his former jailers, who Mandela invited to his inauguration as President, "How did you go without hating them?"[30]

Mandela's response, as reported by President Clinton, was this:

> "Well, you know, I did hate them for a long time, about 12 years. Once day I was out there breaking rocks in prison, and I thought, look what they've taken away from me. They've taken the best years of my life. I can't see my kids grow up. They brutalized me. They can take everything. They can take everything from me but my mind and my

heart. Now, those things I will have to give to them. I don't think that I will give them away."

Clinton went on to ask about that last walk to freedom when Nelson Mandela was finally released from prison, and whether or not he hated those people again. Mandela responded:

> "Yes, I started to. I was also scared because I hadn't been free in a long time; I was actually scared. And I was filled with anger. And then I thought to myself, when I become free, I want to be free. If I still hate them, I won't be free. They've had enough of my time. I'm not giving them any more, not another day."

It's clearly evident that the practice of forgiveness, of living in a state of forgiveness, releases us from the confining bonds of anger, recrimination, self-doubt, and the desire or need for revenge. By practising forgiveness and letting go of the negatives of the past, we can choose to see ourselves positively and take control of our own satisfaction with life. Rather than let our happiness and satisfaction hinge on the acts of others, rather than destroy happiness with a self-defined victimisation, we can choose freedom, peace, and joy for our future.

Following Jesus' Example - Unconditional Forgiveness

There are many passages in the New Testament where Jesus speaks of forgiveness. However, it is the passages where he demonstrates forgiveness that are most moving and most illuminating in our pursuit of a state of forgiveness (Matthew 9:2, Matthew 26:47-56, Luke 5:20, Luke 7:47, Luke 23:33-34, et al.).

> *"Then Peter came to Jesus and asked, "Lord, how many times shall I forgive my brother or sister who sins against me? Up to seven times?" Jesus answered, "I tell you, not seven times, but seventy-seven times." (Matthew 18:21-22)*

In Luke 23 we read the story of the crucifixion of Jesus. In verse 24, Jesus calls to God, *"Father, forgive them, for they do not know what they are doing."*

Christ is speaking not only of those who crucified him, meaning the centurions involved, but broadly, all the people involved, including those who called for his death and the release of Barabbas. In this verse, the Greek word translated as "them" is the word *autos*. Theyer's Greek Lexicon explains:

> "In itself it signifies nothing more than again, applied to what has either been previously mentioned or, when the whole discourse is looked at, must necessarily be supplied."

Got Questions Ministries explains this idea of forgiving all those involved:[31]

> "Even in His agony, Jesus' concern was for the forgiveness of those who counted themselves among His enemies. He asked the Father to forgive the thieves on the cross who jeered at Him. He asked the Father to forgive the Roman soldiers who had mocked Him, spit on Him, beat Him, yanked out His beard, whipped Him, put a crown of thorns on His head, and nailed Him to the cross. Jesus asked forgiveness for the angry mob that had mocked Him and called for His crucifixion (Mark 15:29–30)."

An excellent understanding of the context and importance of this verse is found in a sermon by Charles Spurgeon:[32]

> "OUR LORD WAS at that moment enduring the first pains of crucifixion; the executioners had just then driven the nails through his hands and feet. He must have been, moreover, greatly depressed, and brought into a condition of extreme weakness by the agony of the night in Gethsemane, and by the scourgings and cruel mockings which he had endured all through the morning, from Caiaphas, Pilate, Herod, and the Praetorian guards. Yet neither the weakness of the past, nor the pain of the present, could prevent him from continuing in prayer."

Later in the same sermon, Spurgeon continues:

> "More remarkable, however, is the fact that our Lord's prayer to his Father was not for himself. He continued on the cross to pray for himself, it is true, and his lamentable cry, "My God, my God, why hast thou forsaken me?" shows the personality of his prayer; but the first of the seven great cries on the cross has scarcely even an indirect reference to himself. It is, "Father, forgive them." The petition is altogether for others, and though there is an allusion to the cruelties which they were exercising upon himself, yet it is remote; and you will observe, he does not say, "I forgive them"-that is taken for granted-he seems to lose sight of the fact that they were doing any wrong to himself, it is the wrong which they were doing to the Father that is on his mind, the insult which they are paying to the Father, in the person of the Son; he thinks not of himself at all. The cry, "Father, forgive them," is altogether unselfish. He himself is, in the prayer, as though he were not; so complete is his self-annihilation, that he loses sight of himself and his woes. My brethren, if there had ever been a time in the life of the Son of man when he might have rigidly confined his prayer to himself, without any one

cavilling thereat, surely it was when he was beginning his death throes. We could not marvel, if any man here were fastened to the stake, or fixed to a cross, if his first, and even his last and all his prayers, were for support under so arduous a trial. But see, the Lord Jesus began his prayer by pleading for others. See ye not what a great heart is here revealed! What a soul of compassion was in the Crucified! How Godlike, how divine! Was there ever such a one before him, who, even in the very pangs of death, offers as his first prayer an intercession for others? Let this unselfish spirit be in you also, my brethren. Look not every man upon his own things, but every man also on the things of others. Love your neighbours as yourselves, and as Christ has set before you this paragon of unselfishness, seek to follow him, treading in his steps."

Hanging from the cross, with fresh wounds and incredible pain, Jesus thought was still for those who had sinned against him — those who were persecuting him. What an incredible example of love that is for us to follow! This example that Christ set is a fulfilment of the lesson he provided in Matthew 5:43-48:

> *"You have heard that it was said, 'Love your neighbor and hate your enemy.' But I tell you, love your enemies and pray for those who persecute you, that you may be children of your Father in heaven. He causes his sun to rise on the evil and the good, and sends rain on the righteous and the unrighteous. If you love those who love you, what reward will you get? Are not even the tax collectors doing that? And if you greet only your own people, what are you doing more than others? Do not even pagans do that? Be perfect, therefore, as your heavenly Father is perfect.*

In another sermon by Charles Spurgeon, he explores this verse again, this time focussing on the humble and loving nature of Christ at the end moments of his life:[33]

> "Jesus says not a word in his own defence. When he prayed to his Father, he might justly have said, "Father, note what they do to thy beloved Son. Judge them for the wrong they do to him who loves them, and who has done all he can for them." But there is no prayer against them in the words that Jesus utters. It was written of old, by the prophet Isaiah, "He made intercession for the transgressors;" and here it is fulfilled. He pleads for his murderers, "Father, forgive them."
>
> He does not utter a single word of upbraiding. He does not say, "Why do ye this? Why pierce the hands that fed you? Why nail the feet that followed after you in mercy? Why mock the Man who loved to bless you?" No, not a word even of gentle upbraiding, much less anything like a curse. "Father, forgive them." You notice, Jesus does not say, "I forgive them," but you may read that between the lines. He says that all the more because he does not say it in words. But he had laid aside his majesty, and is fastened to the cross; and therefore he takes the humble position of a suppliant, rather than the more lofty place of one who had power to forgive. How often, when men say, "I forgive you," is there a kind of selfishness about it! At any rate, self is asserted in the very act of forgiving. Jesus take *(sic)* the place of a pleader, a pleader for those who were committing murder upon himself. Blessed be his name!"

The Effort Carries Over - Emotions, Psychology, and Health

The effect of forgiveness is much broader than the focused study of interpersonal relationships (Pastoral Epistles), Christophic/divine forgiveness, and God's love. God has created complex creatures in humanity. One need only look around a busy street to see the variations in physical health and psychology amongst His children. Achieving a state of forgiveness is more than an ideal to strive for, it is a gift of healing and peace that He has provided for us; we only need seek it. This is clearly evident through the positive effects of forgiveness on our psychological and emotional well-being, along with the extended health benefits from letting go of what unforgiveness grasps in its tight little hands.

In an article quoting pastor and author Dr. Michael Barry, we read what he says about the broader effect of forgiveness:[34]

> "Harboring these negative emotions, this anger and hatred, creates a state of chronic anxiety," he said.
>
> "Chronic anxiety very predictably produces excess adrenaline and cortisol, which deplete the production of natural killer cells, which is your body's foot soldier in the fight against cancer," he explained.
>
> Barry said the first step in learning to forgive is to realize how much we have been forgiven by God.
>
> "When a person forgives from the heart - which is the gold standard we see in Matthew 18, forgiveness from the heart - we find that they are able to find a sense of peacefulness. Quite often our patients refer to that as a feeling of lightness," he said.

> Barry said most people don't realize what a burden anger and hatred were until they let them go."

There is definitely a medical aspect prevalent when forgiveness, or lack of forgiveness, is closely examined. The prestigious Johns Hopkins Medicine published the following in regard to forgiveness, or the lack thereof:[35]

> "Whether it's a simple spat with your spouse or long-held resentment toward a family member or friend, unresolved conflict can go deeper than you may realize—it may be affecting your physical health. The good news: Studies have found that the act of forgiveness can reap huge rewards for your health, lowering the risk of heart attack; improving cholesterol levels and sleep; and reducing pain, blood pressure, and levels of anxiety, depression and stress. And research points to an increase in the forgiveness-health connection as you age.
>
> "There is an enormous physical burden to being hurt and disappointed," says Karen Swartz, M.D., director of the Mood Disorders Adult Consultation Clinic at The Johns Hopkins Hospital. Chronic anger puts you into a fight-or-flight mode, which results in numerous changes in heart rate, blood pressure and immune response. Those changes, then, increase the risk of depression, heart disease and diabetes, among other conditions. Forgiveness, however, calms stress levels, leading to improved health."

The well-known Mayo Clinic organisation, which is committed to whole-person care, published the following two lists in regard to the effect of forgiveness on the human body:[36]

<u>What are the benefits of forgiving someone?</u>

Letting go of grudges and bitterness can make way for happiness, health and peace. Forgiveness can lead to:

- Healthier relationships
- Greater spiritual and psychological well-being
- Less anxiety, stress and hostility
- Lower blood pressure
- Fewer symptoms of depression
- Stronger immune system
- Improved heart health
- Higher self-esteem

What are the effects of holding a grudge?

If you're unforgiving, you might:

- Bring anger and bitterness into every relationship and new experience
- Become so wrapped up in the wrong that you can't enjoy the present
- Become depressed or anxious
- Feel that your life lacks meaning or purpose, or that you're at odds with your spiritual beliefs
- Lose valuable and enriching connectedness with others

Citing the work of Toussaint et al., Dr. Susan Krauss Whitbourne, Psychological and Brain Sciences at the University of Massachusetts Amherst, writes in a Psychology Today article:[37]

"Recent research on the health benefits of forgiveness shows that people who can make this mental shift may benefit in ways they didn't anticipate—namely, by living longer."

Her argument is that by substituting negative thoughts of "revenge, resentment, and judgement" with "positive feelings, thoughts, and behaviour" is how we forgive. The end result is a healthier you.

The cited work by Toussaint et al. makes a definite correlation between conditional forgiveness and mortality. Their work concludes with the following statement:[9]

> "Despite these limitations, the present study provides an early glimpse of the potentially important connections between forgiveness and longevity. As an area previously unexamined in forgiveness research, the health consequences of forgiveness and the mechanisms by which its effects translate into measurable impact on mortality risk should receive continued attention. As evidence continues to build indicating the importance of forgiveness in psychophysiological and psychoneuroimmunological processes, health outcomes, and disease, the specific role and pathways of forgiveness in specific- and all-cause mortality risk will emerge."

Forgiveness has become a growing part of psychotherapy since the 1990s.[38] The growing number of research, studies, and publications all point to the effectiveness of forgiveness as part of therapy and counselling. Wade et al. (2013) examined the effect of forgiveness as part of psychotherapy, finding several interesting points:[39]

> "Participants receiving explicit forgiveness treatments reported significantly greater forgiveness than participants not receiving treatment and participants, receiving alternative treatments. Also, forgiveness treatments resulted

in greater changes in depression, anxiety, and hope than no treatment conditions." (p. 1)

"In summary, forgiveness interventions, although not targeting mental health symptoms directly, resulted in reductions in depression and anxiety and increases in hope;" (pp. 10-11)

"First, interventions designed to promote forgiveness are more effective at helping participants achieve forgiveness and hope and reduce depression and anxiety than either no treatment or alternative treatments. Additionally, the specific treatment model used did not make a difference in outcomes." (p. 11)

"For those who are receiving forgiveness treatment, shorter interventions promote less forgiveness than do longer interventions. However, the specific forgiveness model does not seem to make a difference when duration of treatment and modality are controlled. The relationship between duration and effect size also seems to account for other potential moderators such as severity of the offense." (p. 12)

"Another finding of note was that offense severity was positively correlated with forgiveness as an outcome for the forgiveness versus alternative treatment comparisons. One possible reason for this correlation is that a confound exists between severity and duration of treatment. Severe transgressions tend to be treated longer." (p. 12)

"Finally, in the analyses of studies that included follow-up data collection, the overall delta estimating change in forgiveness indicated that on average clients achieve about .78 standard deviations of change at post-treatment and

> maintain that change at follow-up (see Figure 4). Furthermore, these changes appear to persist over time, suggesting that not only do forgiveness interventions help clients achieve forgiveness but that forgiveness is maintained following treatment (e.g., Blocher & Wade, 2010)." (p. 12)

If we are having problems reaching a place of forgiveness for past transgressions against us, then there is no shame in seeking help. My first stop is always prayer, but there have been times when I've needed a more mundane intervention. Therapy can offer real help with this; don't be afraid to seek the help of a sensitive counsellor or psychotherapist/psychologist who can help you work your way to that place of forgiveness. Seeking therapy does not imply any weakness; rather, it implies strength: strength to face the past, strength to face your pain, and strength to face your fears.

The Dark Side of Unforgiveness

While we may understand that not being forgiving, or not forgiving a specific transgression, is against God's will, and therefore sinful, there is a broader dark side to consider and some of it can be confusing.

In the article I previously cited by Todd Morrison, he went on to explain how unforgiveness can have a far-reaching effect in our lives:[25]

> "A life spent practicing unforgiveness toward those who have wounded us feeds that malignant growth in our soul, hinders our capacity for healthy relationships and binds us in the oppressive chains of anger, suspicion, resentment and fear. The residual effect of this cancer of the soul is that it

inevitably targets the healthiest of our relationships. With laser-like precision, our unforgiving ways inflict collateral damage on those we love most, pushing them away from us."

Fr. Al Lauer (1947-2002) was the founder of Presentation Ministries *One Bread, One Body* (daily reflection of the Eucharistic readings for over 32 years) and the radio program/podcast *Daily Bread*. He wrote:[40]

> "When I was first ordained a priest, I believed that over 50 percent of all problems were at least in part due to unforgiveness. After ten years in ministry, I revised my estimate and maintained 75 to 80 percent of all health, marital, family, and financial problems came from unforgiveness. Now, after more than twenty years in ministry, I have concluded that over 90 percent of all problems are rooted in unforgiveness."

In their study on forgiveness and its link to mortality/longevity, Toussaint et al. pointed out a possible danger of forgiveness in the idea of feeling forgiven unconditionally by God:[9]

> "Yet another hypothesis to explore is that feeling unconditionally forgiven by God could lower the likelihood of seeking forgiveness interpersonally. This might reduce social interaction and support and accompanying health benefits, thereby increasing mortality risk."

Personally, I think that the most destructive part of unforgiveness is how it is related to one of the seven deadly sins: pride. Merriam-Webster Dictionary says that a deadly sin is "held to be fatal to spiritual progress."[41] Christian tradition, based on the teachings of the early church, tells us that that the seven deadly sins are: envy, gluttony, avarice (greed), lust, pride, sloth, and wrath.

While you won't specifically find these listed in the Bible, there is an antecedent in the Old Testament in Proverbs 6:16-19:

> *There are six things the Lord hates, seven that are detestable to him:*
> *haughty eyes,*
> *a lying tongue,*
> *hands that shed innocent blood,*
> *a heart that devises wicked schemes,*
> *feet that are quick to rush into evil,*
> *a false witness who pours out lies*
> *and a person who stirs up conflict in the community.*

The concept of the seven deadly sins comes from the original list of *The Eight Spirits of Wickedness* (The original Latin title is: *De octo spiritibus malitiae*). This was a treatise by the 4th-century monk Evagrius Ponticus. He submitted the evil thoughts were: "gluttony, fornication, avarice, sadness, anger (sometimes reversed: anger—sadness), acedia, vainglory, and pride."[42] John Cassian (considered a saint amongst the Eastern Churches) expanded on this work by writing about "the eight principal obstacles to perfection encountered by monks: gluttony, impurity, covetousness, anger, dejection, accidia *(sic)* (ennui), vainglory, and pride."[43] It is based upon these works that the early church derived the current understanding of the seven deadly sins.

The term "pride", biblically speaking, comes from the Old Testament Hebrew words 'ge'ah' (Strong's No. 1344) and 'ga'own' (Strong's No. 1347). Both interpret as pride and arrogance. "Included are the ideas of arrogance, cynical insensitivity to the needs of others, and presumption."[44]

The Holman Bible Dictionary tells us:[45]

> "Some of the synonyms for pride include arrogance, presumption, conceit, self-satisfaction, boasting, and high-mindedness. It is the opposite of humility, the proper attitude one should have in relation to God."

Calvin, Luther, Stott, Lewis and many others tell us that the sin of pride is the great sin, and that, "It is the devil's most effective and destructive tool."[46]

Tony Garland, Th.M., Th.D. writes this about pride:[47]

> "As Christians, we are to recognize that even the tiniest amount of pride (self-exaltation) constitutes sin. Pride, by its very nature, is deceptive and almost always begins as a dangerous, but tiny seed. Rather than saying we are "proud" of our country and our children, wouldn't it be more Biblical to say we are "blessed" or "pleased" with them instead?"

You are probably wondering why I have gone to such a length to expand upon the definition of pride and its origin as a deadly sin. The point is that the original works by Evagrius Ponticus were to counsel other monks[42]. Pride is not only something that lay people contend with, but also those who have devoted their life to God. It's a struggle that we all share. Therefore, we must understand the potency and point of fallibility that pride can bring to us, which is especially magnified when it comes to the topic of forgiveness.

Melissa Miller wrote about the deadly sin of pride for *Canadian Mennonite*, quoting Thomas Aquinas:[48]

> "Pride is such a natural human tendency, and so deadly. "Pride is the first sin, the source of all other sins, and the worst sin," said theologian Thomas Aquinas. Like other sins, pride draws us into ourselves and blinds us to the

> needs of others, and to our place of interdependency in the community."

One of the hidden dangers of being unforgiving in general, or in the specific, is that it can provide us with a dangerous and prideful self-empowerment. The effect can be like a balm to those who question their self-worth, but that balm is a bitter replacement for the sense of value that comes from understanding and knowing God's love for us. This idea is explored in an article titled *Five "Benefits" of Unforgiveness (Then the Better Way)* by pastor and speaker Paul Tripp[49] who suggests that being unforgiving provides us with "dark benefits": power, identity, entitlement, weaponry, and putting ourselves "in God's position."

Have you ever held something over someone's head, or brought up a past blunder against you when it was to your advantage? That's the dark power that you gain from unforgiveness. Remember when I wrote about self-righteous indignation? That's the dark benefit of a superior (prideful) identity you gain. Now I'll ask why you might bring up a person's wrongs from the past: is it to make them feel bad (weaponry), or is it to coerce them into doing something you want them to do (entitlement)? The worst of the five dark benefits of unforgiveness that he writes about is that it puts us in God's position. Pastor Tripp explains it very clearly in his article:

> Debt puts us in God's position. It is the one place that we must never be, but it is also a position that all of us have put ourselves in. We are not the judge of others. We are not the one who should dispense consequences for other's sin. It is not our job to make sure they feel the appropriate amount of guilt for what they have done. But it is very tempting to ascend to God's throne and to make ourselves judge.

Pastor Tripp goes on in this article to tell us why forgiveness is a much better way:

> "It seems almost too obvious to say, but forgiveness is a much better way. The grace of our salvation is the ultimate argument for this truth. Forgiveness is the only way to live in an intimate, long-term relationship with another sinner. Forgiveness is the only way to negotiate through the weakness and failure that will daily mark your relationships. It is the only way to deal with hurt and disappointment. Forgiveness is the only way to have hope and confidence restored. It is the only way to protect your love and reinforce the unity that you have built. Forgiveness is the only way not to be kidnapped by the past. It is the only way to give your relationships the blessing of fresh starts and new beginnings."

Summary

The necessity for a forgiving nature is not only due to the importance placed upon us by scripture, it is inherent to our own wellness and the wellness of the community. The Journal of Humanitarian Assistance published an article that starts by telling us:[50]

> "Once dismissed as an irrelevant religious concept in a political world, the concept of forgiveness has begun to be increasingly associated with highly secular post conflict reconstruction. As the post Cold War *(sic)* world has splintered into violent wars and persistent low level conflict, its potential for healing civil society has begun to be explored in media, popular, and academic analysis. Despite this increased profile, forgiveness may be one of

the least understood and yet potentially necessary acts required for a society to fully break a cycle of violence."

Forbes Magazine used the example of Nelson Mandela to illustrate how forgiveness is a necessary quality in leadership, and how it can move a society forward, rather than have it stuck in revenge:

> "Nelson Mandela famously forgave his oppressors. After the end of apartheid, which had fostered racial separation and kept blacks impoverished, Mandela became South Africa's first democratically elected President. Some in his political party clamored for revenge against members of the previous regime or perhaps even all privileged white people. Instead, to avoid violence, stabilize and unite the nation, and attract investment in the economy, Mandela appointed a racially integrated cabinet, visited the widow of one of the top apartheid leaders, and created the Truth and Reconciliation Commission that would clear the air and permit moving forward."

To you and me, the macrocosm of such sweeping forgiveness is reflected in the microcosm of our own lives. Forgiveness brings us psychological health, emotional healing (whether received or given), and better physical health. Knowing how to forgive and moving through life with a forgiving nature helps us build strong relationships, work through difficulties, and remove the destructive influences of anger, anxiety, and the need for revenge. Ultimately, forgiveness affects our spiritual formation in a very positive way as it helps us grow and remain closer to God. In the end, forgiveness is about, and benefits, *you.*

Actor, director, screenwriter, and producer, Dolf Lundgren, gives a moving talk about forgiveness. He tells about his childhood, being physically abused by his father, and how he left home as a young teenager. Through his life and the work that he did for his own healing, he learned that if you heal yourself, you can heal others. At the end of a talk he gave, he said:[51]

> "Take time to find the little boy, or little girl, inside yourself, treat them well, then maybe you can look at the little boy or girl next to you, you can treat them well. When you do that, it's the greatest feeling in the world."

Chapter 5

Anger

Discussing anger is a very complex topic. There is episodic and chronic anger[52], and pathological anger[53] (anger disorders[54]). The latest version of the *Diagnostic and Statistical Manual of Mental Disorders*[55] (DSM-5) still does not recognize anger, per se, but it does recognize that anger is a contributing part of disruptive mood dysregulation disorder (DMDD, on page 156) as well as intermittent explosive disorder (IED, on page 466); both of which are comorbidities for many other disorders. Anger is also part of schizophrenia (on page 99), delusional disorder (on page 90), and others. People who suffer from anger as a psychopathology have a variety of treatment options available to them[56] in addition to psychological/psychiatric assistance. However, the type of anger that comes from a mental disorder is not what this book is about.

For the purposes of understanding in this discussion, chronic anger is simply recurring episodic anger from the same source/situation or unresolved anger. Therefore, the end goal of this book will address chronic anger as a by-product of addressing episodic anger in the framework of that understanding.

What is anger?

Anger is a neurologically initiated physiological response to a perceived threat to life or safety. That kind of anger is the fight part of 'fight-or-flight': it serves a vital purpose. It prepares us to defend ourselves or others, depending on the situation. Dr. Athena Staik writes:[57]

> "The emotion of anger is a secondary one, meaning it is a cover for deeper underlying fear-based emotions. As such, it serves a useful purpose. When we need to take action to protect ourself, anger is there to block our connection to emotions of vulnerability, or thoughts focused on doubt, lack of control, helplessness, etc., that may otherwise block you from acting to protect our self or another. When our defenses are triggered by our body's "fight or flight" system, this lets us know we perceive a threat to our emotional safety. In this case, anger is our survival reaction. It helps us move past emotions, such as fear, shame, hurt, that can stop us from taking action to meet our needs, both lower needs and higher.
>
> Whereas fear may otherwise paralyze our ability to take action to change a situation, anger moves us to act courageously. This is also valuable in cases where we face obstacles, doubts, fear of failure, etc., and need to stay on course toward meeting our goals."

In my research, I've read several articles relating to the importance and validity of anger. However, they all agree that anger has a purpose, but that purpose is not lashing out at others.[58,59,60,61] The purpose of anger is to alert us to a threat or danger. Thankfully, rather than physical danger, anger is often alerting us to an emotional or psychological danger. It would be a good idea to always remind yourself that you are usually going to have to work towards forgiveness when you feel anger.

Anger, in response to a real or perceived threat, is something that is wired into us as a defense mechanism:

> "Anger is the body's fundamental physiological response to a perceived threat to you, your loved ones, your property,

your self-image, your emotional safety or some part of your identity. The "fight or flight" response prepares your body to fight or flee from a perceived threat to your survival. It is a warning bell that tells you that something is wrong.

First described in the 1920s by Harvard physiologist Walter Cannon, this response is hard-wired into your brain and represents a genetic wisdom designed to protect you from bodily harm."[62]

Summarising an article[63] by Lakeside Educational Network President and CEO, Gerry Vassar, this type of response originates in the amygdala, which is a storehouse for emotional memories. With the input of our senses, the amygdala makes the decision on whether to send the information to the cerebral cortex (the thinking part of our brain) or the limbic system, the emotional centre of the brain. Vassar explains:

> "If the incoming data triggers enough of an emotional charge, the amygdala can override the cortex, which means the data will be sent to the limbic system causing the person to react using the lower part of the brain.
>
> During an overriding event, the amygdala goes into action without much regard for the consequences (since this area of the brain is not involved in judging, thinking, or evaluating). This reactive incident has come to be known as an amygdala hijacking.
>
> When the amygdala is hijacked, a flood of hormones are released that cause physical and emotional alarm. A surge of energy follows, preparing the person for the fight or flight response. The impact of this hormonal flush last for several minutes during which time the person is usually out

of control and may say or do things he or she will later regret, when the thinking part of the brain reengages."

According to Clinical Psychologist, Aaron Karmin, a specialist in anger management, it can take up to 20 minutes[64] for us to return to a state of calmness after experiencing the fight-or-flight response. However, the adrenalin-caused arousal can take hours or days to leave the body[65,63], thus lowering the anger threshold; in other words, making it easier for a person to get angry again. Now you understand why so many things can easily irritate you (dog, kids, spouse, employees, co-workers, parents, etc.) when you are angry about something unrelated to them.

While fight-or-flight kicks in when there is a perceived threat to our physical safety, anger can also be a physiological response to a threat against our psychological or emotional safety. Even with psychological or emotional threats, we will still experience the fight-or-flight response.

Dr. Leon Seltzer writes:[66]

> "Still, in my own clinical experience, anger is almost never a primary emotion in that even when anger seems like an instantaneous, knee-jerk reaction to provocation, there's always some other feeling that gave rise to it. And this particular feeling is precisely what the anger has contrived to camouflage or control."

Dr. Seltzer goes on to explain that the anger response may also be the body's self-defence mechanism kicking in to protect you in situ:

> "In Steven Stosny's excellent book *Treating Attachment Abuse* (1995), which delineates a comprehensive model for therapeutically dealing with both physical and emotional

> violence in close relationships, the author offers a chemical explanation of how anger—in the moment at least—can act as a sort of "psychological salve." One of the hormones the brain secretes during anger arousal is norepinephrine, experienced by the organism as an analgesic.
>
> In effect, whether individuals are confronted with physical or psychological pain (or the threat of such pain), the internal activation of the anger response will precipitate the release of a chemical expressly designed to numb it. This is why I've long viewed anger as a double-edged sword: terribly detrimental to relationships but nonetheless crucial in enabling many vulnerable people to emotionally survive in them."

Psychologist Russell Lemle warns that "whenever our threat emotions (i.e. anxiety and anger) are triggered, accuracy goes right out the window."[67] He explains why that feeling of anger in the alerted brain causes this:

> "The function of anxiety and anger is to viscerally warn of a danger so that we take self-protective measures. To succeed at this task, we're designed to over-estimate threat. The only surefire *(sic)* guarantee that actual risks are never missed is giving ambiguous threats the same credence as definite ones. Better to be safe than sorry. This evolutionary adaptation was vital for survival on the savannah, but it's another story entirely with our relationships."

Anger is the primary protective emotion, designed to protect us from harm or from loss of something of value.[68]

Charles Smith, of Kansas State University, explains the similarity of anger resulting from a threat or from injustice:[69]

> *"Threat.* Anger is always a response to something or someone that takes or tries to take something tangible or intangible of importance to us. We feel angry because we feel threatened. This threat may or may not be true. If we believe it to be true, then we react as though it were in fact a real threat. If we are not threatened, we don't feel angry.
>
> *Perceived injustice.* At the moment of experiencing anger, we believe the threat is unfair. We believe the circumstance is not the way things are supposed to be. At the moment of anger, what we experience as unjust is experienced as real and immediate.
>
> The more angry we become, the greater our risk for distorting the nature of what we view as an unjust threat."

Building on the idea of a sense of perceived injustice, Leland Beaumont puts forward the presence of a "wilful agent" as part of anger.[70] Someone has acted deliberately, or rather, you have perceived that someone acted deliberately, whether the deliberate act was intentional or not. That wilful agent can be a person, an organisation, or even yourself.

Anger comes from fear

If it hasn't become clear yet: *all anger is a result of fear*.

This may be a difficult concept to grasp at first. The difference between anger and fear is that fear makes us want to move *away* from the threat, whereas anger makes us move *towards* the threat.[69]

It is extremely important for you to understand that getting angry does not make us poor followers of Jesus, it has a purpose. Anger is not un-Christian and is not a sin, nor is it behaviour: anger is a response.[71] What we do with the anger, however, is where our relationship with God comes in.

Understanding anger can help us on the path to forgiveness. By understanding anger, and understanding the fear that caused it, we can increase our understanding when examining the event that put us into a state of anger. This helps us to see the situation from another perspective, one that has context and correlation to the actual event that transpired.

Myss and Shealy wrote in *The Creation of Health*:[142]

> "Anger is one of the reactions to fear. When a person or an event threatens you and you become afraid of losing body, life, money, love, or sense a moral injustice: you may react with anger. The next time you are angry, just ask yourself what you are afraid of losing."

It's been my experience, that no matter what I am angry about (mad, pissed off, enraged), it can always be reduced to a response to fear. Learning to do this was not an overnight process. It took me a long time to be able to question myself and get beyond the surface responses. By peeling away the onion of our emotional reaction, we get to the root, but sometimes that takes a lot of peeling, and often, tears. Learning to do this will take practice, though, so be patient.

As you peel away the layers of your emotional/psychological onion, remember that if you haven't gotten to fear, you aren't there yet. So long as your examination includes the word like "they", "them", "he", or "she", then you haven't finished the process. Making sure that you are examining *your* fears is very important to this process of examining your anger.

Once you have gotten to the root of your own fear(s), then you have a basis for perspective shifting.

As I said above, there is nothing un-Christian about experiencing anger as a reaction. How you deal with it is where our faith and the instruction of our Saviour needs to be at the forefront of our thoughts. There is nothing in the Holy Bible that prevents us from confronting someone that has hurt us.

> *"If your brother or sister sins, go and point out their fault, just between the two of you. If they listen to you, you have won them over." (Matthew 18:15)*

However, that confrontation must be done from a place of love, not a place of anger or spite[72].

> *"Brothers and sisters, if someone is caught in a sin, you who live by the Spirit should restore that person gently. But watch yourselves, or you also may be tempted. Carry each other's burdens, and in this way you will fulfill the law of Christ." (Galatians 6:1-2)*

Anger danger - pride

There is a sneaky spiritual danger that accompanies anger at someone. Have you ever waited until *after* you got revenge to forgive someone? Have you ever *delayed* your forgiveness until they had been paid back? Have you ever *held on to the anger* just long enough to make sure they got their just desserts?

When you delay your forgiveness until after you have requital, then you are not being forgiving in the way that the Lord intends for you to be. True forgiveness, unconditional forgiveness, is given without a need for revenge, recompense, or the desire that the perpetrator suffers as well.

In a book about the power of forgiveness, Robert Stermscheg wrote:[73]

> "My wife, even when wronged by a close friend, finds it easy to forgive. For me, I know it's an issue of pride, based on performance. Whenever I've been offended, there's always that part of me that wanted to hang onto the hurt to show I've been wounded."

We have often been told that *pride* is the deadliest sin. Evangelist Harold Vaughan explains the role of pride in corrupting us:[74]

> Pride was the first sin to destroy the calm of eternity. It was pride that cast Lucifer from heaven and it was pride that cost our first parents their place in Paradise. Pride is the first sin to enter a man's heart and the last to leave. No sin is more offensive to God than the sin of pride. Pride has been referred to as the "complete anti-God state of mind." It militates against God's authority, God's law, and God's rule.

If you are delaying your forgiveness until you get an apology (conditional forgiveness), then you are not offering your forgiveness as Jesus has taught us to. If you are delaying your forgiveness until the other person "gets theirs," then you are not truly being forgiving at all. Yes, it can take some time for you to get to a place where you are able to forgive, but don't tarry in your own work to get to that place where you can forgive (Ephesians 4:26-27).

Be honest with yourself, and therefore with God, when you ask yourself if you are able to forgive yet. Are you not yet able to forgive, or are you waiting for the butcher's bill to be paid? Are you not yet able to forgive, or are you enjoying the attention you get as the wounded victim? Are you not yet able to forgive, or are you being encouraged by others not to? Are you not yet able to forgive, or are you putting yourself above God's will?

> *"Therefore if you have any encouragement from being united with Christ, if any comfort from his love, if any common sharing in the Spirit, if any tenderness and compassion, then make my joy complete by being likeminded, having the same love, being one in spirit and of one mind. Do nothing out of selfish ambition or vain conceit. Rather, in humility value others above yourselves, not looking to your own interests but each of you to the interests of the others. In your relationships with one another, have the same mindset as Christ Jesus: Who, being in very nature God, did not consider equality with God something to be used to his own advantage; rather, he made himself nothing by taking the very nature of a servant, being made in human likeness. And being found in appearance as a man, he humbled himself by becoming obedient to death — even death on a cross!" (Philippians 2:1-8)*

It is vitally important that you don't let your anger sit and fester for both the reasons stated previously in this chapter and for your own spiritual health.

> *"In your anger do not sin": Do not let the sun go down while you are still angry," (Ephesians 4:26)*

Matthew Henry's commentary on Ephesians 4 provides us with a very good explanation of how we handle anger and the importance of dealing with anger quickly:[75]

"Take heed of anger and ungoverned passions. *Be you angry, and sin not,*' v. 26. This is borrowed from the Septuagint translation of Ps. 4:4, where we render it, *Stand in awe, and sin not.* Here is an easy concession; for as such we should consider it, rather than as a command. *Be you angry.* This we are apt enough to be, God knows: but we find it difficult enough to observe the restriction, *and sin not.* "If you have a just occasion to be angry at any time, see that it be without sin; and therefore take heed of excess in your anger." If we would be angry and not sin (says one), we must be angry at nothing but sin; and we should be more jealous for the glory of God than for any interest or reputation of our own. One great and common sin in anger is to suffer it to burn into wrath, and then to let it rest; and therefore we are here cautioned against that. "If you have been provoked and have had your spirits greatly discomposed, and if you have bitterly resented any affront that has been offered, before night calm and quiet your spirits, be reconciled to the offender, and let all be well again: *Let not the sun go down upon your wrath.* If it burn into wrath and bitterness of spirit, O see to it that you suppress it speedily." Observe, Though anger in itself is not sinful, yet there is the upmost danger of its becoming so if it be not carefully watched and speedily suppressed. And therefore, though anger may come into the bosom of a wise man, *it rests* only *in the bosom of fools. Neither give place to the devil,* Eph. 4:27. Those who persevere in sinful anger and in wrath let the devil into their hearts, and suffer him to gain upon them, till he bring them to malice, mischievous machinations, etc. "Neither give place to the calumniator, or the false accuser" (so some read the words); that is, "let your ears be deaf to whisperers, talebearers, and slanderers."

Matthew Henry, a non-conformist pastor from the 17th century,[76] is explaining the need for us to deal with anger quickly. If we don't, then there is the chance that we will take action that is rooted in the anger, actions that will be sinful:

> Those who persevere in sinful anger and in wrath let the devil into their hearts, and suffer him to gain upon them, till he bring them to malice, mischievous machinations, etc.

One of the many things he says in this commentary that is valuable to remember is:

> And therefore, though anger may come into the bosom of a wise man, *it rests* only *in the bosom of fools.*

Frustration is like anger

So, you feel angry, but there is no object of your anger (person or entity), but rather it's the situation itself which is frustrating. "Like anger, frustration is a natural human emotional and psychological response to something. The feeling is often due to disappointment when an effort or observation does not work out as expected or anticipated."[77]

The differences between anger and frustration are:[78]

- Frustration is commonly a response to inner conditions and anger is commonly a response towards external conditions. (A person may not automatically get angry, but may get automatically frustrated because it can originate from within)
- Frustration is usually a slow and steady response, but anger is usually a quick and aggressive response.

- Frustration is difficult to be detected in a person's body language and can be easily hidden, although anger, most of the time, is visible and identifiable.

A user on the PsychCentral.com forum explained the difference this way:[79]

> Anger: A strong emotion; a feeling that is oriented toward some real or supposed grievance.

> Frustration: The feeling that accompanies an experience of being thwarted I attaining your goals.

Related to anger and disappointment, frustration arises from the perceived resistance to the fulfilment of an individual's will or goal.[80] How you deal with frustration is the same as how you deal with anger: the root of frustration is fear. So, you need to go through the same process of peeling back the onion to discover the fear of loss that is fuelling the frustration response.

The dangers that accompany frustration are the same as those for fear, but with a twist. Where anger, and your immediate response to anger, is a knee-jerk reaction, repeated frustrations might put a negative response behind a mask of acceptability.

Imagine your goal is to become a team leader in the workplace. Each time you are denied that goal, you commit to trying harder and improving your performance. That's a fantastic response. However, as your frustration grows, you realise that you need to also start pointing out the problems with those who keep getting moved into that position ahead of you. You start making decisions in your work that benefit the organization, but thwart the other person or make them look bad. You talk to others on the team about the team leader, and their poor decisions (that were based on your work or input). You have a "quiet word" with the boss about the person in that position, relaying information with a negative spin. Do you see what is happening here? Instead of being happy for their success, and supporting them with a positive attitude and professional commitment, you are secretly working against them for your own glorification (pride). This response is based on your frustration (fear of not being recognised, fear of not gaining power, fear of not gaining the benefit/recognition through advancement, etc.).

Frustration is insidious in its capacity to affect us slowly, compounding problems through its persistence via repeated frustrations of attaining a goal. Whereas anger can clear up in as little as twenty minutes, frustration can last for months, years, or a lifetime. Some of the effects of frustration can be loss of confidence, stress, depression, abuse of drugs or alcohol, eating and weight problems, and other addictive behaviours.[81]

In a 2010 study published in the *Behaviour Research and Therapy Journal*, Szasz et al. published their research on *The effect of emotion regulation on anger.*[82] Their researchers split the test subjects into three groups, and each group was provided different instructions on ways of handling anger. They were then required to complete tasks that were frustrating (p.116):

> Acceptance: Experience your anger fully as a normal response without trying to control, change it or fight against it in any way.
>
> Suppression: Try not to think of the situation that makes you angry, mad or irritated. Please try as much as you can not to think about the situation, don't think about how you feel or what had happened, and try to suppress your emotions and not feel them. It's very important to try as

much as you can not to think about the situations that makes you angry, mad or irritated.

Reappraisal: Tell yourself that it would be preferable that the others are nice and/or fair to you, but if they are not, it does not mean that you or they are worthless human beings. It would be preferable that the others be nice and/or fair to you, but if they are not, remember that it is only (very) bad, not catastrophic (the worst thing that could happen to you). It would be preferable that the others are nice and/or fair to you, but if they are not, you can tolerate it, and go on enjoying life, even if it's more difficult in the beginning.

The study showed (p. 117) that the difference in anger scores between the *Acceptance* and *Suppression* group were not statistically significant. The *Suppression* group reported more anger than the *Reappraisal* group, and the difference between the *Acceptance* group and the *Reappraisal* group was significant. While the study found no difference between the *Acceptance* and *Suppression* group in regard to task persistence, the *Reappraisal* group persisted significantly longer with the frustrating task used for testing.

This research confirms (p. 118) that in accord with other research, *suppression* is the least effective means of dealing with frustration because it "leads to elevated levels of physiological arousal and psychological distress". The researchers found that the *Reappraisal* method of handling frustration was the most effective. They do concede that this was an examination of short-term response and there is a need for more study over longer-term frustration.

The *Reappraisal* method of responding to frustration reflects what I am putting forward in this book, which you will read in the following chapters. The efforts of others do not mean you are worthless. You cannot control the response of others, but what you can do is: determine your own response; keep things in perspective; through your faith in God's love, you can accept what has happened and move forward, rather than being mired in the self-pity locus of fear.

Dealing with anger in situ

So, your co-worker or your spouse says or does something and, *WOW*, your shoulders tense, your fists want to clench, you feel a tingling in your arms, your stomach flips, your pulse starts throbbing in your head, you feel yourself inhaling deeply or slowing down your breathing ... okay, it may not be quite that bad, but anger has emerged.

In discussing forgiveness, anger, and fear, it's important that you know how to put that doggy back on the porch instead of letting it chase the car down the road.

<u>Take a moment, in fact, take several:</u>

Anger is a neurologically-triggered physical response to a psychological perception of threat. Unless you are in a real and imminent physically threatening situation, then you can take the time to let the initial burst of anger subside before saying or doing something really stupid. Don't deny that you are angry; don't think it will show you as weak. Tell the other person you need a moment, or just walk away if you can. Wait until you can return to a place of calm and clear thinking before you respond. Time will give you the calmness to be able to truly understand what you are feeling about what happened.

Don't jump to conclusions:

Don't assume you know what that other person "really meant" or "what it is they really want". When we are in anger mode, our cognitive biases can become even more profound, especially any Fundamental Attribution Errors (we'll talk about this in chapter 7).

Perspective:

Take a moment to think about the good things in your life. In the grand scheme of your world, how important is what just happened? How realistic of an effect will this have on your life, your family, your relationship, or your work? There are 86,400 seconds in a day, how many more seconds of the day are you willing to surrender to your anger over this? If you stay angry and upset, what exactly will be your net profit by doing so?

Don't go to the gym!

You may think that going and having a workout will help you calm down. While it's true that an endorphin rush can make you happy,[83] there is evidence that exercising while angry can triple your risk of a heart attack.

In a study by the Population Health Research Institute at McMaster University in Hamilton, Ontario, they studied 12,461 subjects in 52 different countries whom suffered a first heart attack. The study found that anger or heavy physical exertion doubled the risk of heart attack. However, combining anger *and* heavy physical exertion tripled the risk of heart attack.

In addition to a heart attack, you may find yourself in a state of *gym rage*. An article from the UK quotes a National Health Service psychologist who said:[84]

> "When you are stressed, your body is ready for action. Sitting in a traffic jam or at your desk is not going to help you deal with it. You need to give it some physical action but this only works up to a point. After a while, you just start to wind the body up again."

However, if you know you are going into a situation where your anger may be triggered, then exercise beforehand can have a very positive effect on reducing the arousal you experience.[85,86]

Rebuke

Is your anger in response to a biblical rebuke? Have you become angry because a neighbour has challenged you for sinful behaviour or for doing something illegal?

> *"Better is open rebuke than hidden love. Wounds from a friend can be trusted, but an enemy multiplies kisses." (Proverbs 27:5-6)*

We might get angry with someone for pointing out our biblical (sinful) failings, or because they know that we have done something wrong. Few things hurt us worse than having our own shortcomings exposed.

> *"Don't have anything to do with foolish and stupid arguments, because you know they produce quarrels. And the Lord's servant must not be quarrelsome but must be kind to everyone, able to teach, not resentful. Opponents must be gently instructed, in the hope that God will grant them repentance leading them to a knowledge of the truth, and that they will come to their senses and escape from the trap of the devil, who has taken them captive to do his will." (2 Timothy 2:23-26)*

The passage above comes from Paul's second Pastoral Epistle to Timothy, his friend, student, and companion whom he had left at Ephesus to take charge of the church there.[87] In this we learn that correcting someone who is errant in their application and understanding of the bible is a necessary correction. In an article about *The Gentle Art of Correction*,[88] Pastor Steven Cole says:

> Whether we like it or not (and we probably should not like it!), we all need to learn how to give biblical correction to those who are in sin or in serious doctrinal error. Without correction, churches and families tend to run into the ditch. In our text, Paul shows Timothy how to carry out the gentle art of correction. It applies especially to church leaders, but it also applies to every Christian, because we all have relationships that require at times, if we truly love others, for us to offer biblical correction. So although it is never a pleasant task, it is a part of biblical love.
>
> There are several reasons that we shy away from correcting others. I've already mentioned the fear factor: we're chicken! One key to overcoming the fear of correcting those in sin or error is to recognize what verse 24 affirms, that if you know Christ, you are the Lord's bond-servant. As such, He will hold you accountable for being faithful to Him. You need to fear God more than you fear people and recognize that obedience to His command to love others requires correcting them if you see them heading for the cliff.

Beware that your anger isn't keeping you from seeing that perhaps, someone is acting out of love, even though you may not see it at that moment. Keep this in mind as you peel away at the emotional onion (next chapter) to get to the root cause of your anger (fear).

Conclusion

Remember that it's okay to get angry; it's a natural reaction within our body. The Bible acknowledges that anger is a normal response, but then goes on to command us to deal with it, lest it gives Satan a foothold. What gets a person angry and the level of anger they feel will be different for each person. What is not different, however, is that anger can be used as a tool to help us recognise that we need to take a step back and give ourselves some space before we act on that anger.

How you react to the anger then becomes a matter of your biblical understanding and your desire to live your life as Jesus taught us, and as God wants for us. At that moment, when you have to decide how you are going to respond to your anger (fear), you need to decide if you are going to respond in a Godly way, or are you going to ignore Him and thus reject His love.

Chapter 6

Fear

Hurt, mad, angry, upset, disappointed, insulted, and betrayed: these are some words that describe how we respond to situations where we see another person's actions as causing us psychological harm or injury. In other words, someone has done something to upset us. So now that we are upset, we need to work towards forgiveness. But, honestly, *why* are you upset?

One of the fundamental understandings you need when working towards forgiveness is to understand what you are upset about in the first place. Some things may seem fairly obvious (e.g. infidelity, physical assault, theft), others may not be so obvious. Don't be deceived by your surface response to a situation. By knowing what is *really* upsetting you, you have a better starting point to work through that difficulty.

Sometimes you are mad at a person, sometimes you are mad at yourself, and sometimes you are mad at God. Pastor Rick Warren assures us that we won't be struck by lightning for telling God we're upset[89]:

> "Some of you are angry with God for things that have happened in your past. He knows it, you know it, but you won't admit it. The starting point is to say, "God, I'm still upset. I'm angry that this happened!" God's not going to fry you with a thunderbolt if you confess your feelings. He already knows how you feel. You just start the healing process by admitting it."

He goes on to outline the process around beginning to heal, the process of getting to forgiveness, and it is to start by knowing *why* you are mad; that is, externalising it:

> "Maybe you're trying to bury your past, but it keeps resurrecting itself. There are triggers everywhere that just keep the memory alive. Your past keeps popping back up because you haven't dealt with it.
>
> Instead of burying the past, you need to close the door on the past so you can move on to the present. Where you've been doesn't matter as much as the direction you're going today. You need to close the door on the past, but there is no closure without disclosure. You can't close that door until you've faced your hurt and shared it with somebody.

He goes on to say:

> Today, you may need to write a letter to God and tell him your feelings. God understands your hurt and pain, and he's waiting for you to talk to him about it. Putting your feelings on paper will help you express your heart to God.
>
> Then, you need to get in a small group. You need at least one person you can spill your guts to and who will love you unconditionally. In a small group, you'll meet someone who will become a close friend and will pray with you through your hurts."

Expressing (verbalising) why you are upset (afraid) is a powerful method of gaining understanding.[90] When we externalise our thoughts into spoken words, our mind makes new connections.

Dr. Sian Beilock of the Psychology Department at the University of Chicago tells us:[91]

"People always say it's good to put "your feelings into words." But is it true? If you think about it, the advice seems somewhat counterintuitive. If you are anxious, scared, or worried about something, is it really going to make you feel better to dwell on this anxiety by speaking or writing about it?

The answer, it turns out, is yes. New research published this month in the journal Psychological Science shows quite clearly that, when it comes to the phobias we have, simply talking about them helps curb negative responses to what we fear."

In my workplace, I sometimes have to teach people how to enter individual employees working information into our payroll system software. This can be a very complicated process that requires several entries for each person depending on what type of schedule they are working or what their duties are for the day. One of the things that I always teach people to do is to first, figure out what the person is doing for the shift (the story of the person's day), and then repeat that "story" of the shift to themselves out loud while they are making the entries.

Invariably, whenever the person articulates that story out loud, they get the entries right. However, while learning, trying to process that story in their head without articulating it out loud leads to frequent errors. I haven't trained a single person on the system yet where this verbalising approach has not been proven to work.

As I said previously, articulating your thoughts out loud allows you to make new connections. When we rely on our internal monologue, we go off in tangential directions far too easily. While we are thinking things over in our mind, there is a lot if sensory input competing for our attention. Other concerns easily creep in and distract that internal conversation. By putting the thoughts into words, you are focussing on those thoughts and are able to refine them with far less distraction than relying on the racing speed of our internal monologue.

By articulating why you are mad, you are able to focus on the anger, and it becomes easier to trace that anger back to its root fear.

Know Why You Are Mad

Figuring out why you are mad is probably the most difficult skill in learning how to change your perspective. Why we are mad is often buried deep inside us and not instantly accessible unless you routinely practice self-evaluation.

Psychologist Dr. Deborah Khoshaba writes:[92]

> Oh, we human beings do weave a tangled web, because of our defensive nature. We learn to conceal our fears from others and to protect ourselves from feeling weak, ashamed, and embarrassed. We are so good at this that sometimes, we even deceive ourselves as to what is provoking us.
>
> Thus, what we say is the reason for our anger may not actually be true. In some ways, cave men had it easier. They knew what they were fighting over. But, you may not know why a coworker, lover, family member or friend is angry with you~ or you with them.

According to Sigmund Freud's structural model of the psyche, the feeling of being "mad" at someone comes from the ego in response to either or both of the superego and the id. Summarising Dr. Christopher Heffner,[93] in Freudian psychology the superego is responsible for our sense of morality and our conscience. This can include basic feelings of right and wrong, fair and unfair, justice and injustice. The Superego is the watchdog of our personal security. What makes the response of the ego difficult to understand is that the driving forces of the id and the superego may not be clearly evident unless you dig for them.

Who we are (personality - ego) and how we see ourselves (identity - presumed ego), is a constant response to our unconscious id and superego. They are unconscious because we are not conscious of their impetus. Borghini et al. wrote that "the Ego, which serves as the executive agent for the mind, mediates the demands of the Id and the Superego."[94]

Because of this, we sometimes need to dig deep into ourselves, peeling back the layers of the emotional onion, to understand our motivations. Peeling back the layers of the onion is what the Jewish philosopher Martin Buber described as, "the world where self is exposed to the self."[95]

What did they do? Why do you think they did it? What did you feel when they did it? Why did you feel that way? What does that feeling remind you of? When else have you felt that way? What things could make you feel that way other than what you are examining? What is the risk issue that this raised in you? Why is that a risk? What are you potentially losing in this situation? Can you really lose that? What is it that you are afraid of? What is it about this that makes you see that loss as worthy of fear? What is the reality of that fear? What happened the last time you faced something like this?

These are some of the questions you will be asking yourself as you move deeper into understanding your motivations and choices. At the root of it, you are going to find a fear of loss. As you face those basic motivating fears, it may be helpful for you to understand a simple truth about "fear": *fear is about what might happen, it is about something that has not yet become a reality.*

Fear is always about something that has not happened

Fear, anxiety, and panic are our projections onto the future; sadness, grief, and hurt come from the past. We become fearful when we consider the reaction or result of something that our imagination has formulated as something that *might* come to pass. As we confront these "fears" of something that has not actually happened, that has only been imagined, stop and think about how many times you have had a fear that was actualized. The answer will be "not very many".

Remember: *fear is about the future; it is about our internal dramatisation of what the future will be.*

I have a great deal of experience in this area: dealing with fear. Doubly challenged with both generalised anxiety (everyone is out to get me) and social anxiety (everyone is judging me), I could say that I have a Hard Knocks University degree in catastrophizing situations that have not yet occurred. One of the mainstays of my therapy to deal with those has been that the F.E.A.R. is "False Evidence Appearing Real". Overcoming fear (anger) is a process that can be learned and practised. This evidentiary examination of what causes my anxiety attacks is what I have described above: asking questions about what you are thinking and feeling, being truthful with your answers about what is going on inside you, and paying attention to what is projection and what is realistic.

Chair of the Criminal Justice Program at the University of California, Al Valdez says to frame every disaster in your life with the words, "In five years, will this matter?"[96]

Psychological Impacts on Processing Fear and Forgiveness

If you are just beginning your emotional growth or having difficulty getting beyond a past hurt and moving on to a place of forgiveness, perhaps you should consider counselling as an adjunct to your prayer work. Sometimes this process of learning about what is going on inside of us can be scary. It may bring up things you aren't yet prepared to deal with. There is no shame and nothing non-biblical about getting professional help from a qualified therapist or psychologist,[97] contrary to what you may hear from those who have never had the strength or clarity of understanding to ask for psychological help.

A psychologically-rooted problem can interfere with your ability to connect with God, prayer notwithstanding. The anxiety, panic attacks, and depression I was dealing with were becoming an interference with my spiritual formation and my relationship with God. It wasn't because I lacked in desire, but because my mind became preoccupied with worldly matters over my faith due to the illnesses. I've lived much of my life, since opening my heart to God, holding tightly to Philippians 4:4-7:

> *"Rejoice in the Lord always. I will say it again: Rejoice! Let your gentleness be evident to all. The Lord is near. Do not be anxious about anything, but in every situation, by prayer and petition, with thanksgiving, present your requests to God. And the peace of God, which transcends all understanding, will guard your hearts and your minds in Christ Jesus."*

By releasing my cares and concerns (*"Do not be anxious ..."*) I was able to stop worrying about things and leave them in God's hands. It never failed that at the end of whatever trouble or concern I had placed in His hands, the outcome was exactly what it needed to be. However, as the mental illness emerged and intensified, I lost the solace of this passage because, while I would put the problem in His hands, I was psychologically unable to let go of it. This wasn't a lack of faith; this was brain chemistry and physiology.

Because the anxiety would not allow me to let go of the problems, I couldn't feel and enjoy the peace from God resulting from the process of letting go. In turn, I found myself thinking less about God's mercy and ability to carry me, focussing instead on the mundane concerns and their possible (imagined) outcomes.

The effect of mental illness on my spiritual formation was one of the reasons that I finally went to my family doctor and asked for help. It was one of the best things that I have ever done for myself and for my relationship with God.

Historically, religion was considered a symptom of mental illness, and the Diagnostic and Statistical Manual of Mental Disorders III (DSM3) portrayed religion negatively by suggesting that religious and spiritual experiences are examples of psychopathology.[98] Thankfully, that is no longer the view of the world of psychology and psychiatry.

Faith, religion, and mental illness have a complex relationship in regard to their effects on one another. I've read articles that say prayer and faith alone will cure mental illness, but I can assure you, from the perspective of my own experience, that attitude is pure *poppycock*.

In an article written by Ed Stetzer for Christianity Today, he says:[99]

> "Among evangelicals, you will find some who are very open to dealing with mental illness as a physiological reality, but you will also find others who think that there is no other value to be gained from listening to the world.
>
> One might wonder why we can't just read enough Scripture or pray enough. Why can't that cure us? Because the reality is that in some cases, there are physical, chemical, or physiological issues. Yes, prayer can help, and yes, God does still heal in miraculous ways. But more often than not, more prayer and more faith are not the only remedy for mental illness. Medicine is still needed."

A *Washington Post* article from 2013 offers this perspective:[100]

> When people suffer despite prayer and consider therapy, "people think: 'Is this a knock against my faith? Am I not believing in God enough? Now I have to resort to this?' "said Henry Davis, leader of the evangelical First Baptist Church of Highland Park. "I believe God is in therapy. I believe God can be in medicine. If someone says, 'I'm just going to pray,' you have to do more."

In a study by Lifeway Research, it was reported that 28% of individuals with acute mental illness agree their mental illness hurts their ability to live like a Christian.[101]

Brandon Cox, pastor and mentor to pastors, writes in his article *What Every Pastor Needs to Know About Mental Illness*:[102]

> "I believe that God is the Creator and Healer of body, mind and spirit. But I also believe that in most cases, He chooses to work through long-term solutions such as medicine or therapy to bring about healing. And I also believe that Satan is alive and real, but I don't feel that every difficulty

I face can be handled by a prayer to bind some particular "spirit." And sometimes I feel that our faith borders on a kind of superstition that puts people in harm's way. For example:

- If you think people with schizophrenia just have demons that need to be cast out ...
- If you encourage depressed people to "just praise the Lord" and forget about their troubles ...
- If you ever urge someone to "throw away their pills" and stop trying to medicate their sin ...

... chances are, you're doing more harm than good. We have the mistaken idea that medicinal treatment for mental illness is somehow a substitute or counterfeit for being authentically who we were made to be. To put it another way, many Christians assume that if you were really right with God, you wouldn't need medication. The truth for many people is that medication is the mechanism that allows them to rediscover who they really are by clearing away the irrational thinking that clouds their minds without it."

The point of this discussion on mental illness and the ability to process our anger is one that I will re-state due to its importance:

- There is no shame in seeking help.
- There is nothing non-biblical about seeking help.
- God can work through the medical professionals in psychology and psychiatry, just like he does the doctor mending you broken bones.

Be Courageous About Examining *Your* Anger to Find *Your* Fear

Finding that root fear takes practice. When I started learning how to do this, I stumbled, and it took lots of practice. It's difficult to ask questions where the answer will reveal your weaknesses. Looking in the mirror of our self-identity (presumed ego) can be frightening in itself. To move forward to a healthy place, a place where fear doesn't control us and forgiveness is in our nature, requires that we take this journey.

If someone gets a promotion ahead of you when you know they didn't deserve it, what are you upset about? Is it that you employer has chosen someone with less skill? Is it that you didn't put your A-game forward when you should have? Is it that you are afraid people will think less of you, or think you are less deserving because you didn't get it? Is it because you were relying on the pay raise that comes with the promotion?

If you get mad at someone for calling you "fat", what are you upset about? Is it because you are ashamed of your body? Is it because you feel like you have failed in your attempts to lose weight? Is it because that statement out loud is calling the attention of others to something that you are sensitive about? Is it because it makes you feel less worthy?

If you find out that your spouse has cheated on you, what are you mad at? Are you angry that the bond of trust was broken? Are you angry that you were so easily fooled by them? Are you upset that this will mean the breakup of the family (financial) unit? Are you afraid to be alone? Are you afraid people will be talking about you and laughing at you? Are you afraid that your sense of power and control over your life has been wrested away from you? Are you afraid of all of them?

If your teenage child sasses you, what are you mad at? Are you afraid you no longer have control over them? Are you afraid their behaviour, if not corrected, will wind up embarrassing you in front of others? Are you afraid that you have lost control of an aspect of your life, that aspect being your power over another person? Are you afraid they are letting go of the apron strings and that your relationship with them is changing?

Peeling Back the Layers

When we apply forgiveness to a situation, there will undoubtedly be some questions in your mind about a person's motivations (the wilful agent). While you may have the good fortune for an honest heart-to-heart discussion with the other person, often you won't; either they are unwilling or perhaps they are no longer available to you. Regardless, seeing things from that other person's perspective is going to help you apply forgiveness.

Peeling back the emotional layers to look at our fear of the future will cause us to examine events of the past. Doing so takes determination:

> "It takes a conscious choice and a willingness to live in the present and let go of the past in order to see myself and others clearly and not through the cobwebs of old thoughts, feelings, and beliefs."[103]

For our own benefit, and to dig into the root fears, we need to go deep into our emotions. For this process, we use the term "peeling the onion." The onion is a metaphor often used to understand the complexity of our emotional layers.

> "The feelings that we notice are not always the core Feelings. What I mean by this is that sometimes we feel something, but there is another Feeling hiding behind it. It's hiding because it might be a Feeling we don't like to

admit to, a Feeling that is unfamiliar or simply because it's just too uncomfortable."[104]

In his blog on life challenges, Will Swan writes:[105]

> "I think of it as peeling an onion, or shucking corn - whatever visual works best for you. You start by realizing that stepping away from a negative thought doesn't really work, especially if it's a recurring thought. You really need to try stepping into it, but you do it in layers. That way you can follow the trail of negative thinking step-by-step to the root cause and deal with the root after you have dealt with everything springing from it."

Let's look at the example of my son and his *times tables*. It's Saturday morning, the sun is shining, the spring weather is warm, and the birds are chirping in the trees. My eleven-year-old son is visiting for the weekend along with one of his friends. I had plans for us that day. A little while after breakfast, as I'm about to tell them to get ready for us to go out, my son makes a comment about his homework.

What homework?

He then pulls a notebook out of his backpack and tells me he has to memorise his "times tables" for math class. So, I ask him to recite a few off for me, so that I can determine how much work he needs to do.

He looks at me blankly.

I ask him how much two times four is: he answers correctly.

I ask him how much three times four is: he looks at me blankly — again.

We spend so much time that morning and early afternoon going over his times tables (recite /memorise them, quiz him, blank stare) that the plans I had went by the wayside. I explained to him about recitation to help rote memorization, but he didn't seem to get it. I helped him go over them, again and again, as my blood pressure (stress, a.k.a. anger) and my frustration (okay, it was anger) increased. A few times my voice was raised, and my frustration (anger) became obvious. By the time we put the book away, he was upset, his friend was embarrassed, and I was both upset (angry at myself) and embarrassed (angry at myself).

Here is the frustrated stream of consciousness that I was going through silently in my mind:

Why is this so damn hard? Why isn't he getting it? Why is he only learning these times tables now at his age? I learned them when I was a lot younger! Why did he wait till now to tell me? Why didn't he tell me last night? Doesn't he respect me? Doesn't he trust me? Am I failing him as a father?

I have plans for us! If we have to sit here all day and do this, we won't be able to go out and do what I wanted us to! How can I connect with him over homework when we could be having fun? Will he only remember this? It's so unfair we can't build a fun memory today. Am I failing to be a good father? Am I failing him as a father?

And why does he keep looking at his friend and laughing? What the heck is so funny about this? Why is this amusing? Why isn't he taking this seriously? Am I doing something wrong? Haven't I taught him right? Am I failing him as a father?

What if his mother finds out I didn't get him to finish his homework? Why do I have to spend Saturday doing this, I only have him for the weekend? How will she react? What will she say?

Will she blame me? Will she say I'm not reliable? Am I failing him as a father?

There's nothing funny about not doing your homework! There's nothing funny about not getting your times tables! Math is easy! Why isn't this easy for him? Is he having problems in school? Is there a learning problem that hasn't been discovered? Is he going to do well in school? Does this mean he's going to have more problems in school? What's his future going to be like if he can't do simple math? Am I failing him as a father?

I'll make a small confession here: I know that math isn't easy for everyone. I wasn't thinking broadly at that moment. I can do my yearly income tax without a calculator and can calculate sales tax at the checkout counter faster than the clerk can punch the numbers in. So, yeah, for me, math is easy, but that thought in my stream of consciousness is evidence of how I was holding on to only one perspective at that moment: *my perspective, and not my son's perspective*. It took me time to accept the perspective of someone else (my *eleven*-year-old son) that math may not be as easy as breathing (this is a cognitive bias called "Curse of Knowledge", something common for educators[106]).

By the time we finished with his homework, he knew some of it, but not all of it. We simply got to a point where his capacity to take in anymore had been exceeded. Perhaps we also reached the point where my capacity to sit there with this unexpected requirement of our time together had been exceeded as well. Of course, I put away my frustration and was as nice and accommodating as I could be for the rest of the weekend, trying to enjoy it as much as possible, but it was still silently stuck in my craw.

Over the next few days, I came back to this experience again and again. My relationship with my son was becoming more distant as he got older, and I knew at some point he would be more interested in spending those weekends with his friends than with his father. I realised I was sad because what precious little time he and I could have together was taken up by homework. I thought that my anger at him not taking things seriously was my fear that he was not going to take it seriously at any point and not do well in school. I was afraid that he and his friend were going to think I was an ass for how I was responding, and truth be told, I was an ass — I just didn't want to face that fact. I preferred to see myself as being correct, strict, right, committed, etc. I was afraid that if he went home on Sunday without his homework being done, then his mother (whom I was not having a great relationship with at that time) would cause problems for me seeing him in the future (she didn't). But these concerns were diversions in my mind, diversions from the most painful of the fears: *the fear that I was failing him as a father.*

At the time, I missed the importance of those hours helping him do his homework. It was time we were spending together when he had the distraction of his friend there for the weekend. I should have seen that homework as a niche of time for "us" that was carved out of the day. I also failed to realise that by focussing on the homework over what had been planned, by concentrating on his education, I wasn't failing as a father; it was, in fact, a moment of success, albeit tainted by my emotions of the moment. After that, when he visited, I always asked if he had homework to do. If he did, I let him complete it without interfering, but made myself available to him for his questions. I never reacted that way again.

I am happy to report that, fifteen years later, the kid who couldn't memorise all of his times tables is now a doctoral candidate working in a cancer research lab. That achievement is all his; he got there by himself through hard work and by impressing those in charge. I'm very proud of him for his achievements not only scholastically, but personally as well. After all, he survived *The Day of The Times Tables* (cue post-apocalyptic music score).

While the process of peeling that emotional onion, the often-scary onion, is a journey that is both difficult yet vital to our wellbeing, there is nothing fun about it. This is especially true when we are challenging our own preconceptions about who we are, our role in the tribe (family and community), and what we have placed value on in ourselves and in life. It's a journey that we must take, but we don't have to take alone. We can do it with an understanding and trusted friend or we can do it with a therapist/psychologist. Ultimately, as I so often do, we can call on Him to be with us through that sometimes-troubling self-examination. Performing this exploration is something that you are never truly going to have to do alone. Ask Him to be there with you, to guide you, to help you understand, and to bring His peace to you as you do the work.

> "Allow God to peel back your layers with you. You will get to know yourself and be able to deal with whatever is hiding deep within the core of your heart. It is not easy and it can be very painful, but it is worth it."[107]

Chapter 7

Knowing Yourself

In the previous chapter, I put forward the importance of being able to examine your anger to find the root fear. That is one of the ways that we learn about ourselves. However, we must expand on this. Having an honest and ongoing understanding of who we are, what we perceive our role in life to be, how we relate to others, and how we relate to the tribe is important not only for our personal growth, but for our spiritual growth as well.

When it comes to the discussion of forgiveness, knowing yourself is also one of the keys to being able to comprehend another's perspective.

Are you a football for other people's opinions? During a Q&A session, Art of Living founder, Sri Sri Ravi Shankar was asked, "Why is it that people who are not on the same path don't understand us and take it against us? I don't understand." His response illustrates the importance of knowing yourself,[108] and it's a valid observation regardless of your religious identification:

> "Let them talk. So what? Take it. It doesn't matter. We don't insist that everyone talk only good. By their talking, you don't become negative.
>
> So, don't be football of others' opinion. Let anybody say anything. It doesn't matter. When you are clear in your heart, and what you do is right, what you want to do is right, you just do it."

When you are a "football for other people's opinions", this means that you allow the prevalent attitude to become how you see yourself or how you think about a topic. If someone says something negative about you, you take that to heart as reality. When a friend or colleague states an opinion, you agree with that opinion rather than state your own. When you operate like this, you allow other people to form your opinions, your view, and your perspective. How can you know who you are, if who you are is defined by others? For some people, having their own view or perspective, their own identity, is a very difficult thing. Nurture doesn't always serve us well when it comes from a bad role model or someone with their own problems. Learning to know your own thoughts, think for yourself, and stand firm for what you believe in is vital to being able to view the perspective of another person, without automatically absorbing that perspective as your own.

The most important part of knowing yourself is to get guidance from our Father who loves us. In his epistle to the twelve tribes, James (brother of Jesus, Bishop of Jerusalem) writes that if we don't understand what it is we are to do or learn from our trials, then we should put the question to God for guidance:

> *"Consider it pure joy, my brothers and sisters, whenever you face trials of many kinds, because you know that the testing of your faith produces perseverance. Let perseverance finish its work so that you may be mature and complete, not lacking anything. If any of you lacks wisdom, you should ask God, who gives generously to all without finding fault, and it will be given to you. But when you ask, you must believe and not doubt, because the one who doubts is like a wave of the sea, blown and tossed by the wind. That person should not expect to receive anything from the Lord. Such a person is double-minded and unstable in all they do." (James 1:2-8)*

Over the years, I have developed a simple process for staying in touch with myself that reflects certain words of hope from the book of Lamentations, chapter 3. This process helps me know who I am, what I am feeling, and what is important to me. Moreover, it helps me see how I have been interacting with others, and whether that interaction is what God wants from me.

Several times a day I will pause for a moment and review the last few hours. I will think about things I've said to people, that people have said to me, situations that I have been in, what I thought and felt, and what I needed to learn from them (if anything) to apply in the future. Of particular importance to this process is recalling what my emotional responses were and what my thoughts were — in the moment. What was my knee-jerk reaction? Why did I react that way? What do I need to learn or understand about myself to improve my reaction to something similar in the future?

Keeping on top of my day, how I'm responding, what I'm feeling, and what the deeper meanings of those things are, helps me *know* myself. It also helps me learn, on a daily basis, to improve different areas. Finally, this is all part of my process for my own spiritual formation, my own process of trying to live in the way that Jesus has taught us to live.

Lamentations is one of the most depressing books in the Old Testament. It is part of the *Megillot*, the five books comprising the third major section of the Hebrew Bible (the Tanakh). This book is a poetic work that laments the destruction of Jerusalem. Chuck Swindoll begins describing the importance of this book with[109]:

> "Like the book of Job, Lamentations pictures a man of God puzzling over the results of evil and suffering in the world. However, while Job dealt with unexplained evil, Jeremiah lamented a tragedy entirely of Jerusalem's making. The

people of this once great city experienced the judgment of the holy God, and the results were devastating."

Chapter 3 of Lamentations speaks of hope for the people of God. After a promise of hope from the past:

> *"Because of the Lord's great love we are not consumed, for his compassions never fail. They are new every morning; great is your faithfulness. I say to myself, "The Lord is my portion; therefore I will wait for him." The Lord is good to those whose hope is in him, to the one who seeks him;" (Lamentations 3:22-25)*

There comes a very important verse a bit further on:

> *"Let us examine our ways and test them, and let us return to the Lord." (Lamentations 3:40)*

When we are dealing with the topic of forgiveness, we are not applying forgiveness to something that was nice, good, or positive. We are applying it to something negative. Lamentations 3 reminds us that in the past good *has* come from God and so there is hope that good *will* come from Him again. Applying this to our own lives in the modern world, we are reminded through this chapter that we have faced challenges and overcome them before, so it is possible to overcome them again. *"Let us examine our ways and test them,"* is about self-reflection on our relationship with God and our understanding of what He wants from us. It is also, inherently, about self-reflection on our own thoughts, feelings, responses, and understanding.

We can find an excellent discussion of this verse in the book *Matthew Henry Commentary on the Whole Bible:*[110]

> "We must set ourselves to answer God's intention in afflicting us, which is to bring sin to our remembrance, and

to bring us home to himself, v. 40. These are the two things which our afflictions should put us upon. 1. A serious consideration of ourselves and a reflection upon our past lives. *Let us search and try our ways*, search what they have been, and then try whether they have been right and good or no; search as for a malefactor in disguise, that flees and hides himself, and then try whether guilty or not guilty. Let conscience be employed both to search and to try, and let it have leave to deal faithfully, to accomplish a diligent search and to make an impartial trial. *Let us try our ways*, that by them we may try ourselves, for we are to judge of our state not by our faint wishes, but by our steps, not by one particular step, but by our ways, the ends we aim at, the rules we go by, and the agreeableness of the temper of our minds and the tenour of our lives to those ends and those rules. When we are in affliction it is seasonable to *consider our ways* (Hag. 1:5), that what is amiss may be repented of and amended for the future, and so we may answer the intention of the affliction. We are apt, in times of public calamity, to reflect upon other people's ways, and lay blame upon them; whereas our business is to *search and try our* own *ways.* We have work enough to do at home; we must each of us say, "What have I done? What have I contributed to the public flames?" that we may each of us mend one, and then we should all be mended. 2. A sincere conversion to God: "Let us *turn again to the Lord*, to him who is turned against us and whom we have turned from; to him let us turn by repentance and reformation, as to our owner and ruler. We have been with him, and it has never been well with us since we forsook him; let us therefore now turn again to him." This must accompany the former and be the fruit of it; *therefore* we must *search and try our ways*, that we may turn from the evil of them to God. This was the method David took. Ps. 119:59; *I thought on my ways, and turned my feet unto thy testimonies."*

This sets an important example not only for our relationship with God, but our relationship with others. Reflection on your actions when you find yourself going against God's word is vital to bringing yourself back to God. So, too, knowing yourself in situations that you have dealt with is vital to being able to bring about understanding and growth in yourself; ultimately, bringing about understanding and growth in your relationship with others.

Building on this, it is important that we know what our relationship is with God. Not our surface platitudes that we offer on Sunday morning, but how we are with Him when we are alone, and no one is watching.

In a series of blog posts, Ted Grimsrud, Senior Professor of Theology and Peace Studies at Eastern Mennonite University, offers this perspective:[111]

> "So much of our spirituality, that which empowers us, stems from how we see ourselves and how we see ourselves in relation to God. My view of human nature is positive. I believe that our journey toward God and our journey toward self-awareness and self-acceptance both go pretty much along the same path. The better we know ourselves, the deeper we look inside, then the better we will know others, and the more clearly we will be seeing God."

Cognitive Biases

As we progress through life, our ego develops *heuristics*:

> "Heuristics are cognitive rules of thumb, hard-wired mental shortcuts that everyone uses every day in routine decision making and judgment."[112]

An illustrative example would be the speeding car analogy:

> "In psychology, heuristics are thinking strategies that guide decisions and judgments that are made quickly. These quick judgments are fueled by learned and readily available information. For example, if a person observes a car speeding toward him, he jumps out of the way without needing to give it much logical thought. This is because the mind draws on past experiences or knowledge (using heuristics) to make the snap judgment to move."[113]

Closely associated to heuristics is *cognitive bias*. While there may be an upside to this (self-preservation requiring immediate reaction), there is a very large downside:[114]

> "A cognitive bias is a mistake in reasoning, evaluating, remembering, or other cognitive process, often occurring as a result of holding onto one's preferences and beliefs regardless of contrary information. Psychologists study cognitive biases as they relate to memory, reasoning, and decision-making. Many kinds of cognitive biases exist. For example, a confirmation bias is the tendency to seek only information that matches what one already believes."

As an example, *confirmation bias* occurs when "people only seek out facts and evidence that conforms to what they already think."[115]

Cognitive biases, according to Dr. Jim Taylor, can be overcome by being aware of them and understanding them:[116]

> "Unfortunately, there is no magic pill that will inoculate us from these cognitive biases. But we can reduce their power

over us by understanding these distortions, looking for them in our own thinking, and making an effort to counter their influence over us as we draw conclusions, make choices, and come to decisions. In other words, just knowing and considering these universal biases (in truth, what most people call common sense is actually common bias) will make us less likely to fall victim to them."

Here are some examples of cognitive biases that may have some play in the situation which is causing you to be angry (afraid):

Anchoring Bias

You listen to a co-worker pitch an idea that you know is lousy, and you can prove it is both wasteful and impractical. However, they do such a good job with the pitch that no matter what data and evidence you have to the contrary, getting that message across becomes an uphill battle.

A worse (experientially) example of anchoring bias is the boss who believes the first person to tell them something. This becomes a problem when people tell the boss something about you, irrespective of facts or evidence to support their claim, and the boss automatically adopts a negative view towards you because of it.

A more destructive example would be someone confidentially telling your spouse that they believe you are having an affair when they have no evidence to support that assertion. The lack of evidence becomes irrelevant as that seed of the idea has already been planted in your spouse's mind.

These situations are examples of the anchoring bias at work. That is, the tendency to accept new information and hold on to it, simply because it is the first piece of information offered.

Harvard Law School's Program on Negotiation describes the anchoring bias this way:[117]

> "Anchoring is a cognitive bias that describes the common human tendency to rely too heavily on the first piece of information offered (the "anchor") when making decisions. During decision making, anchoring occurs when individuals use an initial piece of information to make subsequent judgments. Once an anchor is set, other judgments are made by adjusting away from that anchor, and there is a bias toward interpreting other information around the anchor. For example, the initial price offered for a used car sets the standard for the rest of the negotiations, so that prices lower than the initial price seem more reasonable even if they are still higher than what the car is really worth."

Bias Blind Spot

As if cognitive biases aren't enough to deal with, we also have to contend with our inherent blind spot towards our own biases.

The abstract for a five-experiment research study[118] through Carnegie Mellon University, the City University London, Boston University, and the University of Colorado Boulder provides this explanation in their article's abstract:

> "People exhibit a bias blind spot: they are less likely to detect bias in themselves than in others. We report the development and validation of an instrument to measure

individual differences in the propensity to exhibit the bias blind spot that is unidimensional, internally consistent, has high test-retest reliability, and is discriminated from measures of intelligence, decision-making ability, and personality traits related to self-esteem, self-enhancement, and self-presentation. The scale is predictive of the extent to which people judge their abilities to be better than average for easy tasks and worse than average for difficult tasks, ignore the advice of others, and are responsive to an intervention designed to mitigate a different judgmental bias. These results suggest that the bias blind spot is a distinct metabias resulting from naïve realism rather than other forms of egocentric cognition, and has unique effects on judgment and behavior."

Fundamental Attribution Error

This is also known as the correspondence bias or the attribution effect.

Ever sent someone an email, and the longer you go without a response, the more likely you are to imagine that they are mad at you, being inconsiderate, or some other nasty reason? This has happened to me. "Why the hell am I thinking that?" is a question I've often asked myself while suddenly imagining someone is mad at me, where there are absolutely zero facts in evidence to support that thought. Now I understand why I occasionally experience those thoughts.

It appears, based solely on my own experience, that this cognitive bias is a significant factor in dealing with anxiety, panic, and depression.

Dr. Mark Sherman, professor emeritus of psychology at the State University of New York at New Paltz, explains fundamental attribution error:[119]

> "When we see someone doing something, we tend to think it relates to their personality rather than the situation the person might be in.
>
> For example, if someone cuts in front of you in line, your immediate reaction is, "This person is a complete jerk!" But in reality, maybe he never cuts into lines and is doing it this time only because he is about to miss his plane, the one he's taking to be with his great aunt, who is on the verge of death."

The other side of fundamental attribution error is that while you may perceive someone is treating you poorly because they are a jerk, when you treat someone poorly it's just because you are having a bad day.

Of course, this would all be moot if people would just *answer their darn email on time* ☺

Hindsight Bias

"Hindsight bias occurs when people feel that they "knew it all along," that is, when they believe that an event is more predictable after it becomes known than it was before it became known. Hindsight bias embodies any combination of three aspects: memory distortion, beliefs about events' objective likelihoods, or subjective beliefs about one's own prediction abilities."[120]

Leadnet.org Director of Communication and Design, Tim Nations, summarises the three levels suggested by the authors of that article in which this can manifest itself:[121]

- *I said it would happen* - Misremembering an earlier opinion or judgment about an event or circumstance.
- *It had to happen* - Believing that the outcome was inevitable.
- *I knew it would happen* - Believing that we could personally foresee the outcome.

He explains the two key dangers of this assumption bias:

1. We limit our ability to learn from the past. The more we believe we 'knew it all along', the less likely we are to reflect on why things truly happen. When it comes to strategic thinking, we could find ourselves doomed to repeat past failures.

2. We begin to place too much confidence in our own perspectives. In doing so, we unknowingly begin to narrow our fields of view …. If we really knew it all along, we would have little need for outside perspectives, right?

Observational Selection Bias

So, your spouse gets mad at you when you forget to do something. Suddenly, they're nit-picking everything. Are they unfair? Are they being mean? No, they are simply being human. Being upset about one thing suddenly makes many more upsetting things apparent to us. It's not because they are looking for other things to blast you for, rather, the observational selection bias is throwing those things right into the forefront of their thoughts.

> "This is that effect of suddenly noticing things we didn't notice that much before — but we wrongly assume that the frequency has increased. A perfect example is what happens after we buy a new car and we inexplicably start to see the same car virtually everywhere. A similar effect happens to pregnant women who suddenly notice a lot of other pregnant women around them. Or it could be a unique number or song. It's not that these things are appearing more frequently, it's that we've (for whatever reason) selected the item in our mind, and in turn, are noticing it more often. Trouble is, most people don't recognize this as a selectional bias, and actually believe these items or events are happening with increased frequency — which can be a very disconcerting feeling. It's also a cognitive bias that contributes to the feeling that the appearance of certain things or events couldn't possibly be a coincidence (even though it is)." [122]

Overconfidence Effect

Leadnet.org Director of Communication and Design, Tim Nations, describes this effect:[123]

> "The overconfidence effect is a cognitive bias in which someone believes subjectively that his or her knowledge or judgment is better or more reliable than it objectively is. According to an article in Psychology Today, the overconfidence effect does not deal with whether single estimates are correct or not. Rather, it measures the difference between what people really know and what they

think they know. What's surprising is this: Experts suffer even more from the overconfidence effect than laypeople do."

This cognitive bias is not about egoism or narcissism; it's simply about our own belief that we must be right. The downside of this bias is that we may fail to do the digging, the layer peeling, which is necessary because we don't have any clue or cognition that we might be seeing things incorrectly.

Projection Bias

This particular cognitive bias is quite vital to the understanding around the importance regarding frame of reference and changing your perspective. Projection bias causes us to believe that others are emotionally and mentally processing input and thoughts in the same way that we do. However, this is rarely, if ever, the case. Just because you *think* someone has to know that something is hurtful, mean, or insensitive, does not necessarily mean that they do.

> "The projection bias is a type of cognitive bias that involves overestimating the degree to which other people agree with us. People tend to assume that others think, feel, believe, and behave much like they do. They assume that their way of thinking about something or doing things is typical, and therefor other normal people will respond in a very similar manner.
>
> This is similar to the false consensus effect, in which people overestimate the degree to which other people agree with their opinions."[124]

Semmelweis Reflex

Accepting change can be difficult. Unfortunately, it seems, most of us share an inherent aversion to change. This can contribute to fear, anger, and courses of action that upset others. In the workplace, I've had some vitriolic attacks due to changes that I was spearheading, which I've always attributed to the members of my unit "hating change". In other words, they were expressing their aversion to a new way of doing things which, as it turns out, is only natural because of the Semmelweis reflex. Until now, I've always referred to it simply as "fear of change".

Shawn Herbig, president and founder of IQS Research, describes this cognitive bias:[125]

> "We as humans experience this because we are creatures of habit. We are socialized at a young age to expect the norms of a situation or construct, and it becomes very hard for us to break free of those norms – even if it is harming you or others. This is called the Semmelweis Reflex, and it happens when humans fail to accept new knowledge because it goes against what they believe to be true. The paradigms that we live within, those that define our professional and personal lives, are hard to break down in light of change – and unless that change comes in a manner we can come to accept, then it is very difficult for us to break out of our normalcy. I previously posted on the Affect Heuristic, whereby action is taken contrary to evidence. Here, though, we talk more about not acting at all in light of something new."

Understanding the origin of this cognitive bias brings a clearer understanding, as provided by Dr. Julie O'Toole of the Kartini Clinic for Children & Families:[126]

"Case in point: Ignaz Semmelweis. Never heard of him? If you are a woman you may owe him your life.

Dr Semmelweis was born in 1818 in Hungary. He was an obstetrician who was tormented by the high death rates of women in childbirth from what was then called puerperal (childbed) fever. It struck him that women died more frequently giving birth in the hospital than they did giving birth in the streets. The more famous the physicians, the worse the outcome. How could this be? Eventually, after much experimentation, he introduced the simple measure of having the delivering doctors wash their hands in an antiseptic solution before examining a woman in labor. This concept of hand-washing was based on his theory that "contagion" was the origin of this terrible disease. (Please keep in mind that this was before Louis Pasteur proved germs existed and could cause illness, a fact of life and health that we now take absolutely for granted). The death rate among women in Semmelweis' *(sic)* hospital plunged to an unheard-of low level.

Wikipedia describes what happened subsequently: 'Despite various publications of results where hand-washing reduced mortality to below 1%, Semmelweis's observations conflicted with the established scientific and medical opinions of the time and his ideas were rejected by the medical community. Some doctors were offended at the suggestion that they should wash their hands and Semmelweis could offer no acceptable scientific explanation for his findings. Semmelweis's practice earned widespread acceptance only years after his death, when Louis Pasteur confirmed the germ theory and Joseph Lister, acting on the French microbiologist's research, practiced and operated using hygienic methods, with great success. In

1865, Semmelweis was committed to an asylum, where he died at age 47 after being beaten by the guards, only 14 days after he was committed.'"

Being aware of cognitive biases helps us compensate for them. To overcome them, Stacey Colino, an award-winning freelance reporter, has this to say in regard to cognitive biases that affect your health care, but can be applied in any situation:[127]

"If you want to make better health-related decisions, the first step is to cultivate awareness of various cognitive biases you may have so that you "can guard against them," advises Jennifer Blumenthal-Barby, an associate professor of medical ethics at Baylor College of Medicine in Houston. "Patients can ask themselves: If the information were framed differently -- in terms of mortality [rates] instead of survival [rates] or absolute risk instead of relative risk reduction -- would I still feel the same way or make the same decision?"

It also helps to "look for evidence to support the opposite of what you're thinking," Marsh says. "Ask yourself: Am I considering other options, challenging my own beliefs or thinking through the probabilities?" Discussing these questions with people you trust can help. So can considering how your future self might feel about this decision, Blumenthal-Barby says, "since we know people have a present bias and tend to discount the future." To that end, you might ask yourself: Would my future self resent the choice I'm inclined to make right now?"

Knowing yourself is not only vital to forgiveness, it is also vital to defining who we are when we look in the mirror, and when we present ourselves to others. Defining strong and healthy boundaries comes from the ability to understand ourselves, grow as a person, and ultimately, have a very clear sense of who we are; as well as understanding that who we are will often change over the course of our life in many ways. People change, it's that simple. By staying committed to reflecting on yourself, especially in the aspects of your relationship with God, you will find a path to strength, courage, and probably most important: humility.

Chapter 8

Empathy

"Be kind and compassionate to one another, forgiving each other, just as in Christ God forgave you." (Ephesians 4:32)

Another important ability we need to have in our pursuit of forgiveness is empathy. Empathy is the ability to understand and share the feelings of others; specifically, understanding emotions from another's perspective.[128] It is something that we are born with. A study published in the *Infant Behavior and Development* journal in 2011 showed that all of the test subjects, aged eight to sixteen months, displayed empathy for another person they perceived as being injured.[129]

I found an excellent explanation of empathy in biblical terms in *Watchtower Magazine*:[130]

> One dictionary says that empathy is the "identification with and understanding of another's situation, feelings, and motives." It has also been described as the ability to put oneself in the other fellow's place. So empathy requires first of all that we comprehend the circumstances of someone else and second that we share the feelings that those circumstances provoke in him. Yes, empathy involves our feeling another person's pain in our heart.
>
> The word "empathy" does not appear in the Bible, but the Scriptures do refer indirectly to this quality. The apostle Peter counseled Christians to show 'fellow feeling, brotherly affection and compassion.' (1 Peter 3:8) The

> Greek word rendered "fellow feeling" literally means "to suffer with another" or "to have compassion." The apostle Paul recommended similar sentiments when he exhorted fellow Christians to "rejoice with people who rejoice; weep with people who weep." Paul added: "Be minded the same way toward others as to yourselves." (Romans 12:15, 16) And do you not agree that it would be practically impossible to love our neighbor as ourselves if we did not put ourselves in his place?
>
> Most everyone has a degree of natural empathy. Who has not been moved when seeing heartrending images of starving children or distraught refugees? What loving mother can ignore the sobbing of her child? But not all suffering is readily discernible. How difficult it is to comprehend the feelings of someone who is experiencing depression, a concealed physical impediment, or even an eating disorder—if we have never had such problems ourselves! Nevertheless, the Scriptures show that we can and should develop fellow feeling toward those whose circumstances we do not share.

In an article about the neuroscience of empathy in Psychology Today, we learn that empathy appears to be an inherent skill that is wired into us, but that its response can depend on how fast that response is required:[131]

> "In a study published in the Journal of Neuroscience on October 9, 2013, Max Planck researchers identified that the tendency to be egocentric is innate for human beings – but that a part of your brain recognizes a lack of empathy and autocorrects. This specific part of your brain is called the the *right supramarginal gyrus*. When this brain region doesn't function properly—or when we have to make

> particularly quick decisions—the researchers found one's ability for empathy is dramatically reduced. This area of the brain helps us to distinguish our own emotional state from that of other people and is responsible for empathy and compassion."

The article goes on to illustrate tests that show that empathy is difficult in situations where a person is experiencing emotional states of their own. However, this goes to a point made earlier that forgiveness is not usually something we can apply instantly. It takes time to get there; just as it takes us some time to be empathetic to the person with whom we are involved in an emotional response.

For those who feel they have low levels of empathy, however, don't be alarmed. Empathy is something that we can reclaim or improve:[131]

> "Because our brain's neural circuitry is malleable and can be rewired through neuroplasticity one's tendency for empathy and compassion is never fixed. We all need to practice putting ourselves in someone else's shoes to reinforce the neural networks that allow us to 'love thy neighbor as thyself' and 'do unto others as you would have them do unto you.'
>
> There are no easy answers for how to elevate people's consciousness and empathetic response. I am optimistic that through daily choices of mindset and behavior that anyone can rewire his or her brain to be more empathetic. As with everything, we need to take a multi-pronged approach. Other research has shown that compassion can be trained through: rigorous mindfulness training and/or loving-kindness meditation; physical activity that puts your

body and mind in touch with "disagreeable" experiences some would consider to be a "suffer-fest"; and giving back through prosocial behavior and volunteerism.

Many studies have shown that mindfulness meditation that includes LKM (loving-kindness meditation) can rewire your brain. Practicing LKM is easy. All you have to do is take a few minutes every day to sit quietly and systematically send loving and compassionate thoughts to: 1) Family and friends. 2) Someone with whom you have tension or a conflict. 3) Strangers around the world who are suffering. 4) Self-compassion, forgiveness and self-love to yourself.

Doing this simple 4-step LKM practice literally rewires your brain by engaging neural connections linked to empathy. You can literally feel the tumblers in your brain shift and open up to empathy by spending just a few minutes going through this systematic LKM practice."

To understand the importance of empathy, Lori Freeland explains it quite well in an article about her initial response to the diagnosis of acute lymphoblastic leukemia for her ten-year-old son.[132] She writes about the fact that she received a tremendous outpouring of support from friends and family was amazing, but nothing they did made the slightest dent in her wall of panic and despair. It wasn't until another cancer mom came into the room, sat with her, and said, "My son was diagnosed with leukaemia 10 years ago. He's healthy, happy, getting ready to graduate college. Planning his wedding ... Treatment was hell, but we made it to the other side as stronger, better people. You will make it through. You will survive. No matter what happens, you can do this."

Lori describes her response to this:

"I burst into tears of hope and relief. The crush of an enormous weight I didn't even know I'd been carrying lifted enough to let me catch a full breath.

So what was the difference between that one visit from Ann, and the constant stream of visits from our family and friends? Why were Ann's words able to bring comfort when no one else's had?

Sympathy versus empathy.

Our family and friends came out of love, bearing the right motivation, wanting to help. But they didn't get it. They didn't feel it. Not to the depths that my husband and Kyle and I did. We were stuck in the gritty trenches of childhood cancer. From the ledge above, they watched us with sorrow and pity.

Ann dropped down into our ugliness. Ann understood leukemia. She understood Kyle. She understood me. She'd lived those first days. Survived them.

Knowing I wasn't the first mom to sleep in a cot with a death grip on her son's hand—agonizing over how long we had together—knowing I wasn't alone, penetrated my wall of panic and despair.

When we look down into someone else's trench and feel sorrow and sadness, that's sympathy. When we jump into that same trench and get dirty, that's empathy. The basic idea comes down to commiseration versus identification."

Research into the effect of empathy on forgiveness shows a definite link between the two in that empathy facilitates forgiveness, though it is not necessarily a requirement. Dr. Leyla Ulus from Turkey writes in an international research journal:[133]

"As it will be found out in this literature information, those individuals who learn the forgiveness process and internalize the forgiveness concept act with empathy, tolerance and remedial feelings instead of vindictiveness, self-pity, anger and aggression which are qualified as negative feelings, and this leads to some relief in mental health and psychological terms (McCulloug, Bellah, Kilpatrick and Johnson 2001, p.601). Research made advocates that view that the processes of empathy and forgiveness work together (Norton, 2009; Kmiec, 2009; Berry, Worthington, O'Connor, Parrott and Wade, 2005)."

In a study by McCullough et al., they found a link between forgiveness and empathy[134]:

"Forgiving is a motivational transformation that inclines people to inhibit relationship-destructive responses and to behave constructively toward someone who has behaved destructively toward them. The authors describe a model of forgiveness based on the hypothesis that people forgive others to the extent that they experience empathy for them. Two studies investigated the empathy model of forgiveness. In Study 1, the authors developed measures of empathy and forgiveness. The authors found evidence consistent with the hypotheses that (a) the relationship between receiving an apology from and forgiving one's offender is a function of increased empathy for the offender and (b) that forgiving is uniquely related to conciliatory behavior and avoidance behavior toward the offending partner. In Study 2, the authors conducted an intervention in which empathy was manipulated to examine the empathy-forgiving relationship more closely. Results generally supported the conceptualization of forgiving as a motivational phenomenon and the empathy-forgiving link."

In the author's abstract for the study *Toward Forgiveness: The Role of Shame, Guilt, Anger, and Empathy*, published in the *Counselling and Values* journal, Konstam at al. discovered:[135]

> "Explored forgiving and its relationship to adaptive moral emotional processes: proneness to shame; guilt; anger; and empathic responsiveness. Gender differences associated with forgiving were analyzed. Participants were 138 graduate students in an urban university. Results revealed that guilt-proneness was positively related to Total Forgiveness, as were Empathetic Concern and Perspective Taking."

Referring to a study by Macaskill et al. in *The Journal of Social Psychology*, empathy is once again correlated to forgiveness:[136]

> "According to the present findings, the women scored higher overall than did the men on empathy, but there were no gender differences on overall forgiveness scores. Despite the difference in empathy scores, the findings suggest that, among both men and women, individuals with higher levels of empathy find it easier to work toward forgiveness of others, but not necessarily toward forgiveness of themselves. This distinction is, perhaps, somewhat obvious, given that empathy involves concern with others; nevertheless, the distinction is important because it allows researchers to continue to make theoretical distinctions between those two aspects of forgiveness. The present findings reflect the clinical literature that suggests that individuals tend to make harsher judgments of themselves than of others (Beck, 1989; Walen, DiGuiseppe, & Wessler, 1980). Notwithstanding that speculation, our findings suggest that

emotional empathy is positively correlated with forgiveness of others, but not with forgiveness of self."

The presence of empathy, while not mandatory for forgiveness, makes the process inherently easier. Empathy and the ability to see a situation from another person's perspective has always been a key component in my own pursuit of the state of forgiveness that I want to have in my life. Not only is that desire psychologically sound, and experientially validated, it's also presented to us through scripture.

We find the importance of empathy in different passages in the Bible. In his epistle to the church in Rome, Paul writes of love in action. In this, he says:

> *"Bless those who persecute you; bless and do not curse. Rejoice with those who rejoice; mourn with those who mourn. Live in harmony with one another. Do not be proud, but be willing to associate with people of low position. Do not be conceited." (Romans 12:16)*

"Rejoice with those who rejoice; mourn with those who mourn" is a stirring call to empathy, to sharing the joys and tribulations of those around us. It's through doing this that we, *"live in harmony with one another."*

If you aren't sure about your level of empathy, consider your level of compassion. The Bible shows us that compassion and empathy go hand in hand (though they are not the same thing):

> *"If anyone has material possessions and sees a brother or sister in need but has no pity on them, how can the love of God be in that person?" (1 John 3:17)*

> "Finally, all of you, be like-minded, be sympathetic, love one another, be compassionate and humble." (1 Peter 3:8)

> *"When Jesus saw her weeping, and the Jews who had come along with her also weeping, he was deeply moved in spirit and troubled." (John 11:33)*

Emotional intelligence (EI) is an important component of empathy and being able to view a situation or event from a different perspective. There are many definitions of emotional intelligence, but what it boils down to "is the capacity to reason about emotions and emotional information, and of emotions to enhance thought."[137] It's important to understand that EI is not a quality (e.g. agreeableness, optimism, happiness, calmness), it is a *skill* that we use to understand ourselves and to understand others. The ability to discern an emotion by looking at someone's face and understanding how a person responds to an emotion are examples. Being able to recognise what emotion you are feeling, and then investigate the response that you label with that emotion's name (e.g. happy, sad, angry, betrayed, etc.) is also considered emotional intelligence. Dr. John Mayer, co-founder of the emotional intelligence concept, says:[138]

> "Personal intelligence is the capacity to reason about personality as a whole—including our motives, emotions, thoughts, values, and self-control.
>
> Why is personal intelligence important? Because we use our personal intelligence to solve problems about ourselves and about other people, including our loved ones—and what could be more important than competently resolving problems that concern the people we care about?"

Frame of Reference

A component of empathy is the ability to have an understanding of that person's frame of reference. In the book *Forgive To Live: How Forgiveness Can Save Your Life*, Tibbits and Halliday write about the importance of a larger frame of reference:[139]

> "Most of us use too small a frame. We focus on a single, hurtful event and, based on that narrow perspective, make generalizations about everything else. We never see the big picture. Our lives revolve around a limited part of the total picture and we miss a larger, more meaningful perspective of life.
>
> Forgiveness, however, allows you to change the story of your life by reframing your picture of the past. With empathy helping you understand the hurtful event from the other person's perspective and with humility helping you acknowledge that you have made similar mistakes, you will begin to see your story in a different light. By reframing your story, you change your memory of the past and so free yourself from its chains."

They go on to provide the following illustration of the benefit of broadening your frame of reference:

> "Imagine, for instance, that your best friend says something hurtful about you to someone else. If you focus only on that one conversation — if you give the event a small frame — you are able to view your friend only in that hurtful context. Then you can't help but see your former friend as an enemy, for only an enemy would say such a terrible thing.

A larger frame, however, would remind you that this person has been your friend for many years. What she recently said does not fit with everything she has said before. As you use this larger frame for the picture of your friendship, you remember many good things she has said about you. You see that this one event doesn't match other prats of the picture. And, having placed her remark in this larger context, you don't conclude that your friend has become your enemy. Instead, you ponder how to approach her in order to better understand what she said. *After all, you think, the statement must have some context that I have not yet seen.* Asking your friend for clarification can be much more productive than accusing her of being no friend at all.

Clearly, when you use a larger frame of reference for your picture of the past, you see the person who hurt you as both good and bad rather than as exclusively evil. Yes, what she did in that situation was bad; but even as you realise that, you also see some of the good things about her. If you frame the hurtful event with an even larger frame, you can begin to see her history. You take into consideration some of the circumstances that might have caused her to be the way she is and act the way she does.

Be open to discovering a new way to think about the person who has wronged you. What in his life could have caused him to act the way he does? Maybe he's a perfectionist. Perfectionists have a habit of being overly critical, and they tend to offend the people they criticise. But if you understand that this person is being critical to try to compensate for what is missing in his own life, such as never receiving recognition or praise for his efforts, you realize that his negative comments have little to do with your shortcomings and a lot to do with his inner sense of inadequacy. Only as you gain this perspective can you see some good in him and recognized what he is dealing with. The hurtful incident is not all about you."

Forgiveness is important not only for a spiritual formation, but it is also important in its power to define how we live our lives. It can be a requirement for big things or for small things. Regardless of the cause of our misery, willingness to understand the other person's frame of reference is vital, in most cases, to finding that ability to apply forgiveness.

When we chose to love God, we inherently choose to be forgiving. When we choose to follow Jesus' example in our lives, we choose to practice forgiveness. When we choose to love a person, the state of forgiveness is inexorably going to become something you need. Ultimately, our own satisfaction with life will come from putting the words of our Master and Teacher into practice, whereby one of those things we need to learn is the ability to truly forgive another person, not just pay lip-service to it.

Chapter 9

Changing Your Perspective

> *"Finally, all of you, be like-minded, be sympathetic, love one another, be compassionate and humble. Do not repay evil with evil or insult with insult. On the contrary, repay evil with blessing, because to this you were called so that you may inherit a blessing." (1 Peter 3:8-9)*

Anytime I need to apply forgiveness, there is a change in perspective that occurs to go along with it. In some situations (very minor upsets) it happens for me *almost* immediately, yet in most situations, it takes some time. In my workplace, the management team that I lead know that when they say something that is challenging, I need to walk away and process it for a while before I respond. As we have seen, it takes time to be able to process information calmly and rationally. The effects of the fight response (anger), prevents us from being rational and clear-headed during that initial knee-jerk reaction phase.

Understand your anger, and then understand the fear that created it: How realistic is that fear? How often have your past fears been fully actualized? How did past fears relate to the reality of the outcome in those situations?

Understand the fear in relation to loss: begin peeling the emotional onion and move beyond your cognitive biases. Is that potential loss realistic of fear-driven fantasy? If that loss were real, how would you deal with it? Is it likely that the loss you have imagined could really come to pass?

Understand the effect that this fear response is having on you physiologically: do you feel the stress of it? Do you feel tension? Is your heart rate elevated? Do you have a headache? Are you gritting your teeth? Wouldn't it feel better if you let go of all of that? Holding on to your anger only has a detrimental effect on you; it does not affect the other person physiologically.

Understand the other person's frame of reference: Can you talk to them about this situation? Can you deduce what their fear might be? Can you understand that the other person may have a multitude of stressors that are preventing them from thinking carefully through the situation as well? Remember that the other person's anger, like yours, comes from fear. Can you find a sense of compassion for that person that goes above and beyond your own self-protective responses?

Understand the ownership of emotions: what the other person is feeling that has driven their action is about them, it's not truly about you. Their actions are based on their internal thought process, their emotions, their wants, their fears, their methods of handling day-to-day life. They, too, have a history of experiences that have shaped this experience. They have their own onion that they may be dealing with.

Be the helicopter: take a step back from the situation for a moment. "As we pull back from an emotional situation, we can start to see things much more clearly and rationally."[140] How would others be affected by this situation? What would an outsider's perception of this situation be?

Jim Dincalci, the author of *How to Forgive When You Can't: The Breakthrough Guide to Free Your Heart & Mind*, provides tips for the "helicopter view" by suggesting that you turn the situation around and ask yourself the following:[141]

- How would an impartial observer see this?
- Have I done the same thing to another or to myself?
- Is this similar to a pattern in my family?
- Has something like this happened to me before? Am I reliving a situation I've gone through before, but with different players?
- What can I learn from this?
- Can anything positive come from this? Am I stronger or more resourceful as a result of this having happened?
- What do I get by holding on to this resentment? Who benefits and how?
- Am I keeping the situation alive by refusing to let go?

That entire process of working through my anger, fear, ownership of emotions, and the helicopter view is an illustration of how I change my perspective. I get myself into the state of mind (working through anger and fear) where I can take an honest look from that other person's perspective, and at the situation as a whole. Seeing things from their perspective also means taking into appreciation that person's circumstances, struggles, life condition, etc.

The forgiveness occurs when I choose to express the love that God fills me with, through compassion, understanding, and a desire to heal for all those involved (myself and the wilful agent). Sometimes I express the forgiveness out loud, but sometimes I can't because of the situation; this doesn't change the quality of intensity of the forgiveness that I feel.

How we see our lives, how we interact with others, and how we respond to situations all come from our perspective. It is our perspective on life that defines how we operate as members of our community and our family: our tribe.

Self-knowledge/self-understanding, emotional intelligence, empathy, time, and desire are all part of the understanding that helps us travel the road to forgiveness through the landscape of mutable perspective. These are all things that we naturally have or can learn. The effort that we make to set ourselves up as a forgiving person not only honours God's desire for us and the example that Jesus set, it makes us happier people who contribute to the world in a positive way.

Examples of How I Have Changed Perspective

<u>The Date</u>

About a year after I was separated from wife, I went on a date. It was someone I had met on a website. We had emailed a few times and talked on the phone a couple of times. When we finally met face to face, not long into the conversation, she said, "I only came to meet you because I wanted to see what kind of loser had been married three times and still expected someone to be interested in him."

Yes, she *really* said that — to my face.

So how do you think I reacted? At first, I was pissed off, but as I rode the bus after leaving, I had time to think about what had happened and what I knew of her. In our conversations she had seemed nice, I hadn't detected a mean streak. She had also been quite honest with me, opening up about past hurts and challenges. She had gone through a bitter break up a few months before. Not that long ago, her family had dealt with her father's announcement that he had been living a lie all his life and that he was transitioning to become a woman (transgender). This was something that had troubled her greatly, and she still had not fully resolved her feelings about her father. She also worked in a high-pressure job in the financial industry.

It became apparent to me that I couldn't stay mad about it. What she had said had stung, but the point is that it stung me, not her. If I stayed angry/mad/upset about it, that would also be stinging me, not her. I recognised that she had a full plate of her own and that she seemed to be quite unhappy with several parts of her life. I'm sure there would be a detailed and in-depth psychological explanation for what she said or why she said it, but I realised she was simply sharing her pain (in an unfriendly way) to make herself feel better. With so much in her life that she perceived as difficult, it made her feel better to make someone else feel worse. Realising this, *how could I remain upset with someone who was probably hurting worse than I was?* Her words stung me for a few moments, but her own life challenges stung her every day. I also realised that what had transpired had absolutely zero impact on my life. Her words were not going to change my situation, they were not going to make my situation worse, and no one had heard her words. At that moment, I found that forgiveness was my only option. Looking at the larger perspective, what she had done was a very small thing in relation to the many facets and difficulties in my life at that time. All of these thoughts about her and what she said released me from the negative effects of holding onto negative thoughts, thus allowing me to forgive her.

What I did was change my perspective of both her and the situation.

The Noisy Neighbour

A few years ago, I lived in an apartment building in downtown Toronto. One of the tenants wound up having the police at her door a few times due to noise complaints. That tenant blamed me for having the police at her door because I worked for the police service. She launched a smear campaign against me. She started telling other tenants *this and that* about me, things that weren't true. She even went to my landlord with complaints that were unfounded. He spoke to me about the stuff, but he was taking it with a grain of salt. A few weeks into this, the landlord came and told me that one of the other tenants had spoken with him to advise he was the one that called the police on my neighbour. Finally confronted with the truth, she stopped her harassment, but refused to apologise for her hurtful actions.

You would think I would have been mad about this, well I was — initially. Over time I learned more about this neighbour. She had mental health problems, a poor relationship with her family, and money troubles. Having the police at her door was, culturally, a source of shame for her. She needed to protect her sense of identity and try to claim some twisted sense of control in the situation. After thinking things through, I knew that I could not stay mad at her and that I had to apply forgiveness. Why? *Because she was just being who she was.* I realised that she couldn't help but lash out at someone in that situation she found herself in - she wasn't equipped to see her own actions as being responsible for having the police at her door. Was it wrong of her? Yes. Was it mean-spirited? Maybe. Was it going to affect her at all if I didn't forgive her? No. Was it going to affect *me* if I didn't apply forgiveness? Yes! Realising that she was operating in a manner that was the only way she knew how to respond was freeing for me. It helped me find that forgiveness for this situation.

In other words, I changed my perspective.

Divorce

Infidelity can cause a marriage to end in a blaze of hurt. When I found out my wife was having an affair, I felt like I had been smacked in the face with a 2x4, that I had been gut-punched, and that the whole world was going to be laughing at me. I tried everything in my power to save that relationship. After a few weeks, we reconciled and moved forward. Fast forward four months, she was having another affair. At that point, the marriage was over by mutual choice.

During that experience, I remember spending about six hours curled up in the corner of the bedroom, on the floor, crying non-stop. My entire world had crashed down on me. All the hopes, plans, and dreams that I had for the future had been ripped away from me. My entire sense of self-worth had been called into question. I had wrapped so much of my self-identity around the relationship that when that relationship was taken away, I had no clue whom I was anymore. I remember that day on the floor, crying, quite clearly. I remember how mad I was, how much I hated her, and how much I hated what had happened.

Those hours spent on my knees, in tears, was a very important experience for me.

During that time, I thought about everything that had happened, all the hurtful words that had been said (by both of us), and of the many things that had transpired in our relationship over the years. I came to a new understanding in those hours. She had said at one point that she felt like she was drowning: she was in a relationship that had gone too far, when she never wanted to be in it in the first place. After we had gotten together, she didn't know how to break it off as she was afraid people would laugh at her for choosing poorly. When she had walked down the aisle on our wedding day, she had to fight the urge to turn and run out the door. She had gotten to the point that she could barely stand being in the same room with me, let alone look at me, and yet she knew that the situation she was in was her own doing. Yes, she powered on through it because she was afraid of something worse. She had not only wasted four years of my life, but she had also wasted four years of her own life. She simply got to a point where she knew she couldn't go on, yet she didn't know how to make a change. In the end, I had asked her why we reconciled briefly. She said it was because she was more afraid of being alone than what she suffered internally by staying with me.

In those hours on the floor, with tears coating my face, I came to a new understanding of the woman that had been my wife. For the first time, I had enough information to see her life through *her* eyes. As I did this, I realised that all those things I questioned about myself (self-worth, self-identity, and hopes for the future) were about me, not about her. I had control over those things. I knew that I was a good person. I knew that I was a capable person. I knew that my identity was my own, and was not dependent on someone else.

I also realised that she was hurting as bad as I was, perhaps worse, but in a different way. I knew that she hated that she hurt me. I knew that she had tried to make things work in her own mind. I knew that the end of our marriage was not about me, it was about her needs. I knew that it was not that there was anything wrong with me, nor was there anything wrong with her. It was just what it was. She had reached a point that she could not continue with it anymore through the crushing emotional hurt.

Love, real love, is unconditional. Just like God's love for us, love for another person is either without condition, or it is not real love. This woman that I had loved was hurting. If I was mad and spiteful, hating her, then where was the love in that? As I dried the tears and finally picked myself up off the floor, I realised that the love I felt for her was real and therefore, I was compelled to act in a loving way. One of the ways we act in a loving manner is through forgiveness. She never asked for forgiveness, I never told her it was offered, we never spoke that word to one another; in fact, we haven't spoken in almost two decades. However, my heart became settled with the peacefulness that forgiveness brought me that day.

But what was the catalyst for that change in attitude, that understanding and eventual application of forgiveness? I had changed my perspective.

The Needy Neighbour

A few years ago, I lived in a small community. My neighbour came to me one day and asked to borrow some money, so I lent it to him (Matthew 5:42). A couple weeks later he came and asked again, building on the story he gave me the first time. This went on for a while, and each time he asked, I gave, because I had it to give (Matthew 6:19-21). However, there came the point where I just couldn't give anymore. A few months later I woke up one morning to find that he had moved, no forwarding address, and no repayment that he had promised me. I was out $2,230 and knew I would never see it again.

I learned a valuable lesson through this, but probably not the one you are thinking. Had I had the money, I would have leant him more. I knew he was in a bad financial spot, and although I realized he was feeding me a line, I also knew what Jesus said in the Sermon on the Mount: I had given to the one who asked me, and not turned away from the one who wants to borrow when I was able to share. Am I mad at him? No, I'm not. He was being who he was; doing what he needed to survive. I wasn't the only one he "borrowed" from. I know that he wasn't asking for the money for luxuries, he needed the money for basic subsistence. I would have probably scrounged a little harder if he had been honest with me, but I don't hold any animosity towards him. If I saw him on the street today I'd greet him with a smile and not even mention the money (Luke 6:30, 34). Do I feel like a doormat? Not at all; I was simply following the teaching of Jesus.

In the end, I had changed my perspective.

The Car Accident

A few years ago, I was in a minor car accident. I was slowing down, my signal was on, and as I was about to turn into a plaza parking lot, I was rear ended. My first response was a very loud expletive. After making sure the other driver and passenger were okay, the anger started to build. Because of the laws where I lived in Ontario, the police don't have to come to minor accidents; you just exchange information and then go to a collision reporting centre. After exchanging info and making my way there, I was in a ripe state of self-righteous anger by the time I arrived. I was so mad that I was locked in a subjective loop and I couldn't be objective over what had happened. Over the next few days, however, I came to understand where that anger came from: fear.

If the insurance companies determined I was at fault or partially at fault, then my insurance rates would go up (I wasn't, and they didn't). I was afraid of how much a rate increase would impact me financially (there was no financial impact). I was going to need some repairs done to my car. My deductible is $1,000, and I knew that I would be on the hook for that if any portion of the fault was assigned to me (it wasn't, I didn't have to pay the deductible). I drive a jeep because the high seat is much easier on my lower back, which I've injured in the past. I was afraid that while my car was in for repairs, I would have to drive a rental that would be difficult for me physically (the car rental turned out to be a crossover with a high seat base). I lived for over a decade without a vehicle, until I was finally able to afford one. To have it damaged because of someone else's carelessness was so eminently unfair when I worked so hard to get and keep the car (my sense of fairness had been attacked - superego).

In this list of things that made me angry, every single one of those has a root cause in fear. To summarise Myss and Shealy:[142] my anger was a fear-based reaction. But the truth of the situation didn't stop there. I needed to take a step back. The person who rear-ended me was on her way to the grocery store with her eight-month-old daughter in a car seat in the back of the car. As she was braking behind me, also planning on turning, the child woke up with a scream. That startled the mother, and she turned to look at her infant child. At that moment, her foot came off the brake slightly, and the collision occurred. The woman was not careless or an unsafe driver: she reacted to the wail of her child, something which I could understand and would have done myself.

In reality, the accident was no one's fault: it was truly accidental. Was that woman responsible for my fears? No, she was not, my fears are my own. Was she negligent for caring about her child? Absolutely not. I could see, over the course of several days that my anger was unwarranted. Not the initial anger, which was a physiological response, but holding on to the anger was unwarranted. Once I understood my own fears (anger) and took the time to look at the situation from her perspective, I was able to let go of the anger (fear) and be forgiving about what had happened. Did she ask for forgiveness? No, she didn't need to. By coming to the point of forgiveness, I was able to let go of all the negative associations I had with the incident, return to a place of calmness inside, and move forward with the incident behind me and no longer affecting me. The forgiveness was not about her, it was about me.

In getting mad at the woman driving the car that hit me, my ego was using anger to process the fear that I was subconsciously reacting to.[143]

The ability to change your perspective, that is, step back and see a situation more broadly, is vital to forgiveness and to existing in a complicated world. Understanding our cognitive biases helps us with the process. While our own views are important, taking the time to appreciate the view of another person will help us in the pursuit of freedom, peace, and love that forgiveness will bring to us.

Chapter 10

Forgiving Yourself

"One cannot forgive oneself any more than one can kiss oneself." - David Den Haan

Forgiving yourself is the most difficult of all forms of forgiveness, and there is a reason for that: *it is not possible to forgive yourself.*

Wow — I bet you didn't expect that.

Just to be clear, and to remove any ambiguity in that statement, I'll say it again: *it is not possible to forgive yourself.*

The first thing we need to do is to really understand what it is we mean when we talk about "forgiving yourself". I can't really think of any way that we can transgress against ourselves unless we are speaking existentially, which would be a whole different book. The Bible talks about two kinds of forgiveness: divine forgiveness and interpersonal forgiveness. Interpersonal forgiveness is between *two* people; two *different* people. Therefore, when you are seeking a manner to deal with your guilt, it is not forgiveness that you are seeking from yourself.

What you are seeking is a release from the internal bondage you have placed yourself in with guilt, regret, recrimination, etc.

Why the idea of *self-forgiveness* is the wrong approach

In our pursuit of forgiveness of others, I have talked a lot about psychology and the mind. One thing that psychologists teach us is that forgiving ourselves and moving on is vital for a healthy existence. However, I must take exception to this, for fundamental biblical *and* experiential reasons.

When we read the Holy Bible, we will not find a single passage about self-forgiveness. Old Testament or New Testament, it doesn't matter, you won't find it anywhere. Yes, there are lots of passages, valuable passages, about forgiveness between people. The Bible often speaks about forgiveness from God and interpersonal forgiveness. Many have tried to interpret those passages in terms of *self-forgiveness*, but such interpretations dishonour both the word of God and God's intentions for us.

Reverend David Den Haan explained this in a sermon:[144]

> "Would it surprise you to hear that scripture says absolutely nothing about forgiving yourself? There is not one word or verse or even description of anybody coming to terms with the pain in his or her own life by forgiving him or herself. The notion of "forgiving oneself" may sound kind of biblical but there is, in fact, nothing in Scripture about it. There is a lot of information about and examples of and commands to exercise forgiveness, but the Bible always presents forgiveness as a relational issue--something that takes place between two parties who are in relationship with one another. One cannot forgive oneself any more than one can kiss oneself.
>
> There are people who have tried to find a biblical background for the practice of forgiving oneself but the passages that they mention are all about the forgiveness

that God gives to us or the forgiveness that we are called to give to one another. Again, there is nothing in the Bible about forgiving oneself!"

The reason that we won't find any passages, allegory, metaphors, or concepts of self-forgiveness is because of one fundamental truth that applies to Old Testament and New Testament passages: as sin is an offence against God, only God or Jesus (Matthew 9:1-8) can forgive sin.

So, let's put on the brakes for a moment. You are probably wondering why it is we need to be forgiving or *seek* forgiveness from others if it is only God or Jesus who can forgive sin. The answer becomes clear if you take a step back and look at the whole picture (frame of reference).

- Sin is a transgression against God, for which we seek and have been granted forgiveness.
- When we hurt someone (victim), we are having an effect on our neighbour (the victim), whom we are to love as ourselves, and it was most likely a sinful act.
- Therefore, we seek forgiveness from God for our sin, but we seek forgiveness from our neighbour for hurting them; conversely, we can grant forgiveness for being hurt by them, but we cannot grant forgiveness for their transgression against God.

Is it clear now how the idea of self-forgiveness is not a valid approach? Only God can forgive sin, not man. Only the person who is hurt can forgive that hurt, not us. Self-forgiveness is either a prideful heresy in that we think ourselves more important than God, or we are dishonouring the neighbour whom we had harmed by our presumptive position of arbiter of forgiveness when we were the one that acted harmfully.

Pride is the stumbling block

The fact that it is impossible to forgive ourselves, however, doesn't mean that we have to live with the internal bondage that recrimination for our past actions places upon us. That mental prison where we replay events over and over, holding on to deep and profound regret for our decisions or actions that hurt someone (or were contrary to the teachings of our Saviour) is something that I think all of my readers will have experienced at some point. It's a crushing and destructive experience; one that can follow us throughout our lives because we don't truly know how to deal with our past actions.

For years I pursued "self-forgiveness", only to find it frustratingly elusive. So many nights I spent on my knees (literally and figuratively) asking God to forgive me, over and over, because I knew that I could not forgive myself. Because of some things in my past, I wound up pursuing self-destructive behaviours to punish myself in an attempt to atone for my past. I was even able to convince myself that God wanted me to engage in those behaviours as punishment, although study and understanding have revealed that was simply self-delusion as to the nature of God's love.

Author and Pastor Rick Thomas addresses that previous behaviour of mine this way:[145]

> "In some cases with some Christians, they have a difficult time receiving and resting in God's full forgiveness. They may even ask God to forgive them multiple times, but the lingering residual feeling of conviction remains. This feeling is a false sense of guilt that is not resting in the transformative power of the Gospel.

Their lack of Gospel trust disables them from fully appropriating the undeserved favor He provides. These unbelieving Christians (Mark 9:24) continue to struggle with ongoing issues like guilt, remorse, shame, and embarrassment.

Their self-imposed guilt may even drive them to isolate from others by hiding the real truth about what is going on. Like their predecessor Adam, they cover themselves with fig leaves.

Then the eyes of both were opened, and they knew that they were naked. And they sewed fig leaves together and made themselves loincloths. – Genesis 3:7 (ESV)

Hiding unresolved guilt issues complicates the original sin with other sins they pursue to find relief from the guilt. Rather than running to God, they entangle themselves in a godless orbit of temptations that pushes them into a spiral of self-perpetuating dysfunction."

Alexander Pope published *An Essay on Criticism* in 1711. In this work, one line stands out because the quote and its variations have become so widely known: "A little learning is a dangerous thing."[146] We can actually learn more by expanding on that original quote from the book-length poem:

> A little Learning is a dang'rous Thing;
> Drink deep, or taste not the Pierian Spring:
> There shallow Draughts intoxicate the Brain,
> And drinking largely sobers us again.

Bill Morelock, co-founder of the Bob & Bill classical radio show on Minnesota Public Radio, explained the importance of these four lines in an article on the Classical MPR website:[147]

> "The Pierian Spring was a source of knowledge sacred to the Muses, in the shadow of Mount Olympus. It's a peculiar liquor. Sipping is the sin. Binging, in the sense of immersion, is the responsible behavior, taking one beyond giddy enthusiasm to a been-there, done-that wisdom. So the danger in my little learning, it appears, is analogous (there I go again) to being drunk and disorderly."

My pursuit of self-forgiveness came from a little bit of knowledge *because I had drank shallowly of God's word*. I assumed that what all the psychologists and self-help gurus talked about, self-forgiveness, was actually possible. As I began working on my spiritual formation, immersing myself in study and understanding of God's word, it slowly became evident as to what I was doing wrong: putting myself ahead of, or above, God. As I began studying and understanding what Jesus teaches us, and what God tells us, I found that *"drinking largely sobers" my understanding*.

In pursuing *self-forgiveness*, I was putting myself *ahead of God*: I was engaging in the deadly sin of "pride". This act of putting myself ahead of God, of usurping the role of God in my life, was heretical, blasphemous, and prideful. It took a while to wrap my head around that. This was partly due society and psychology's assertion of how important it is to forgive myself.

The heretical nature of this approach can be seen in William Stewart's book *An A-Z of Counselling Theory and Practice*:[148]

> "In counselling, the client may be looking for absolution for some wrongdoing — real or imagined. Part of forgiveness is being able to accept forgiveness from God and from other people. Just as relevant are clients being able to forgive themselves — to act as their own God, to mete out absolution and justification, particularly where the

> forgiveness is not related to some religious omission or commission …"

> "… When working with self-forgiveness, help the client to find a part of self that can act as a forgiving, all-loving God, who will offer absolution. In the entry on Psychosynthesis there is a section on subpersonalities; a study of this, and of using imagery, may well show a way in which the client can create a subpersonality who can act as internal priest."

Here is the problem with this approach to self-forgiveness: *to act as their own God.*

Sue Bohlin writes in her blog on bible.org:[149]

> "I've also heard Christians say, "I know God has forgiven me, but I just can't forgive myself." It sounds quite humble, but in reality, this is upside-down pride. The underlying message is, "God may have forgiven me, but my own standards of what constitutes forgiveness are higher than God's, and my standard is what counts."

There is only one God. When you attempt to act in His place, you are putting yourself above Him. Therein lies the root cause of trying to forgive yourself being the wrong approach. When we are forgiven by God, our sin is washed away, and we can put *the need for forgiveness* behind us. We, however, cannot wash away our own sin, as Christ already did that for us at Calvary.

That, unfortunately for the human brain, is a major stumbling block: *putting it behind us.*

How can we put the memory of our actions behind us, forgiven or not, when we keep going over it in our minds? There are things we have done that we will hold onto for years, perhaps our entire lives, regretting and hating ourselves for it. We ask God's forgiveness and intellectually we know it is supposed to be given, but if it has been given, why do we still feel so bad about it for so long? How can there be forgiveness, Godly or not, if we are still mired in the recrimination, self-disgust, and despair — our internal bondage — caused by our actions?

There is a three-part answer that we will be exploring: humility, confession, and repentance.

Dealing with the Internal Bondage

If forgiving ourselves is a sin, then how do we deal with that self-destructive monster of internal bondage we are subjected to by our regret over our actions?

In a word: *humility.*

Leslie Vernick, of the Association of Biblical Counselors, explores this:[150]

> "Before someone can experientially accept God's grace, she must emotionally (not merely intellectually) accept who she is. There is only one God, and she is not him. She is a creature: one who is called both saint and sinner, beautiful and broken. Humility is the only path that will give her the internal freedom she craves because once she is humble—Jesus called it "poor in spirit"—she'll be in a position to emotionally accept who she is—a fallible, imperfect, sinful creature who doesn't know it all. Then, she will no longer be so shocked, shamed, or disappointed when she sees her darker, sinful, weaker side"

Remember the words of Rick Warren about being humble from chapter 3:[19]

> "True humility is not thinking less of yourself; it is thinking of yourself less."

When we keep a humble spirit in regard to our past misdeeds, we can accept our actions without trying to rally a defence for that internal monologue of regret and recrimination. It happened, *accept* that it happened; *accept* that you are at fault for what you have done. Once you *accept* it and stop fighting it, you can then move forward.

Our Sin as a Learning Opportunity

Accepting His divine forgiveness and dealing with our own recriminations are two different things. There are things that I have done in my life for which I have accepted God's forgiveness and that I no longer beat myself up over. I will also never forget that I did them or how others were hurt by my actions; nor do I want to forget it.

The memory of these things humbles me. They remind me how easy it is to find myself facing regrets and recriminations. These memories make me more careful about the choices I make in my life as I move forward through the years. These memories, and understanding the impact of my actions, make me more compassionate for victims of other people's actions; it also makes me more understanding and compassionate of those who have hurt others (including me). These memories helped me eventually acknowledge that I am an alcoholic, and it is those memories of the hurt that I have dealt others that keep me from taking a drink.

The first step in moving forward is *confession*. You have asked God for forgiveness, but do you really know what it is that you are being forgiven for? When we seek forgiveness from God, we must first confess our sin to Him through prayer. In a sermon on Lamentations 3:28-29, Charles Spurgeon said this about confession:[151]

> "It means, first, that there must be true, humble, lowly, confession of sin. You say that you have been praying, yet you have not found peace; have you confessed your sins? This is absolutely necessary, confess your sins to me you ask? No, thank you; I do not want to hear your confession. It would do me much harm, and it could do you no good to tell them to me; it is to God alone that this confession should be made. Some men have never really made a confession of their sin to God at all; they have done it in such general and insincere terms that it did not amount to a confession. Go you, enter your chamber, shut the door, and get alone; and there, with words or without words, as you find it best, acknowledge before God your omissions and commissions, what you have done and what you have not done. Pour out the whole story before God, and cry with the publican, "God be merciful to me a sinner." Do not cloak or dissemble before the Almighty. Let all your sins appear. Take a lowly place; not simply be a sinner in name, but confess that thou art a sinner in fact and deed. I do believe that some of you are in darkness much longer than you need to be, because you do not stoop to a humble confession of your sin. Let the lances into this ugly gathering of yours that brings you so much inflammation of mind and pain of spirit. Let your confession flow like water before God; pour out your heart before him. Own to your

sins, take the place of a sinner, for this is a great way towards finding salvation: "If so be there may be hope."

Further than that, dear friends, when it is said that we are to put our mouths in the dust, it means that we are to give up the habit of putting ourselves above other people, and finding fault with others. How often is the value of our penitence destroyed because we have looked at Mistress Somebody, and said, "Well, I am guilty, but still,-well, I am not such a hypocrite as Mrs. So-and-so." What have you to do with her? "Oh!" says another, "I know I have been a bad man, but then I-I-I have never been as bad as old So-and-so." What have you to do with him? Here are you pretending to be humble, yet you are as proud as Lucifer. I know you; you are like that man who went up to the temple, and pretended that he was going to pray, and then he said, "God, I thank thee that I am not as other men are," and so forth;" nor even as this publican;" turning his eye in disdain towards the true penitent. There is many a man who says, "I am a sinner, but then I am a total abstainer and wear the blue ribbon; that is a good thing, is it not?" Yes, it is, but not if you trust in it for salvation. "Oh, but!" says another, "I know that I have not lived as I ought, but I have always paid 20s. in the pound." So ought every honest man, but what is there to be proud about in that? Are you going to get to heaven by paying 20s. in the pound to a man, and not a penny in the pound to God? Yet that is often the way of men. Or else perhaps we are accusing others while we pretend that we are ourselves humble. We must get rid of all such bad habits if we want the Lord to have mercy upon us. I believe a sincere penitent thinks himself to be the worst man there is, and never judges other people, for he says in his heart, "That man may be more openly guilty than I am, but very likely he does not know as much as I do, or the circumstances of his case are an excuse for him." A woman, convinced of sin, says, "It is true, that woman has fallen, and her life is full of foulness; but perhaps if I had been tempted as she was, and had been deceived as she was, I should have been even worse than she is." Oh, that we might all give up that habit of caviling at other people, and put our mouths in the dust in self-abasement before God!"

Confess your sin — own your sin. Before God, take full responsibility for what you did and then, humbly and earnestly, repent. You repent by expressing your regret and remorse for the other person's suffering, or for disobeying the instruction you have been given. This is the first step in receiving forgiveness. This is how we ask God for His merciful forgiveness. This is how we begin breaking those internal bonds that we have placed on ourselves.

Breaking those internal bonds to the past also means we have to do work on ourselves, but it has to be work based on our faith and a proper understanding of the value of humility. After we have confessed our sin to God and repented for our actions, it's time to begin healing inside. That healing begins by approaching our internal struggle with as much humility as when we bowed our head before God.

The Great Commandment can be found in all of the Synoptic Gospels (Matthew 22:37-40, Mark 12:29-31, Luke 10:25-28).

> *"Jesus replied: "'Love the Lord your God with all your heart and with all your soul and with all your mind.' This is the first and greatest commandment. And the second is like it: 'Love your neighbor as yourself.' All the Law and the*

Prophets hang on these two commandments." (Matthew 22:37-40)

We can find an antecedent to this in the Old Testament book of Leviticus:

"Do not seek revenge or bear a grudge against anyone among your people, but love your neighbor as yourself. I am the Lord." (Leviticus 19:18)

We also find this reiterated in Paul's epistle to the churches in southern Galatia that struggled with legalism:[152]

For the entire law is fulfilled in keeping this one command: "Love your neighbor as yourself." (Galatians 5:14)

So, what does the Great Commandment have to do with freeing ourselves from internal bondage and humility?

Everything.

Paul's focus on the Great Commandment in his letter to the southern Galatian churches (Antioch, Iconium, Lystra, and Derbe[153]) is very important for us to understand. The churches of southern Galatia "were converts from paganism (Gal 4:8–9) who were now being enticed by other missionaries to add the observances of the Jewish law, including the rite of circumcision, to the cross of Christ as a means of salvation."[154]

Whereas legalism provides for eternal life through a checklist of actions to curry favour with God, *"Love your neighbor as yourself"* reinforces "the total sufficiency of Christ and of faith in Christ as the way to God and to eternal life, and the beauty of the new life of the Spirit."[154]

Going back to the Great Commandment, *"Love your neighbor as yourself"*, remember that it is a command — *period*. It is not a suggestion; it is not optional.

So, what does *love your neighbor as yourself* have to do with humility and letting go of the detrimental thoughts anchored in our past? Charles Spurgeon delivered a sermon (No. 145) titled *"Love Thy Neighbour"*. This is an incredible view of what that means and what it looks like day-to-day; I urge you to Google that sermon and read the entire text. Here are two points from it that I want to share:[155]

> "It is not enough for you to say, you do not hate your neighbour, you are to love him. When you see him in the street it is not sufficient that you keep out of his way, and do not knock him down. It is not sufficient that you do not molest him by night, nor disturb his quiet. It is not a negative, it is a positive command. It is not the not doing, it is the doing. Thou must not injure him it is true, but thou hast not done all when thou hast not done that."

> "Dear friends, remember that man's good requires that you should be kind to your fellow creatures. The best way for you to make the world better is to be kind yourself."

In Paul's epistle to the church in Ephesus, he writes this as part of his instruction on Christian living:

> *"Get rid of all bitterness, rage and anger, brawling and slander, along with every form of malice. Be kind and compassionate to one another, forgiving each other, just as in Christ God forgave you." (Ephesians 4:31-32)*

So here is where we can begin to free ourselves from that internal bondage, leave the past in the past, and move forward without that destructive focus on our failure(s). If we are to love our neighbour, we are to do so with great compassion and without negativity.

Therefore, if we are to treat our neighbour in this way, we must also treat ourselves in this same manner. Remember, Jesus commanded to *"love your neighbor as yourself"*. This means that the destructive, despising, accusatory, and demeaning ways in which we think of ourselves must be set aside. We have been forgiven by God, but now we must move forward in His love and relief, knowing that we cannot undo our mistakes, nor ever forget them.

Using humility to move forward from our past actions

We may be angry at ourselves for our past actions. If we are, we need to deal with that anger by finding out what the root cause of our fear is, our fear for ourselves and our future, *and then acknowledge that fear to ourselves.*

If we are sad because of what another has experienced due to our actions (or inactions), then we need to *acknowledge* that sadness as a positive aspect of ourselves, our empathy. *We need to acknowledge to ourselves* that the sadness is due to compassion for the suffering of another person; even if that suffering was a result of something we said or did.

The words or actions cannot be taken back, they cannot be revoked, there is no reset-point that we can jump back to, and we cannot travel through time and undo that which we have done. *We need to acknowledge to ourselves* that we are powerless to change what transpired in the past; however, we must also *acknowledge to ourselves* that we are able to affect how *we* deal with this moving forward.

Because of our desire to be forgiven by God, and because of our understanding of our wrong-doing, we need to *acknowledge to ourselves* that we have the opportunity to learn from this experience. We can learn about how we deal with situations (the event that caused your internal bondage), we can learn about how we respond to our own fallibility, we can learn how to deal with a similar situation in a more positive and productive way in the future. *We need to acknowledge to ourselves* that there is a lesson to be learned in what has transpired.

It is imperative that *we acknowledge to ourselves* that God wants us to free ourselves from these wounds, even if we have caused these wounds. His love and mercy for you are profound and without comparison. If you don't let go of your grip on the past, or that grip that the past has on you, then you are once again putting yourself above Him. If God has forgiven you, why do you feel the need to keep punishing yourself?

With these acknowledgements and our humility, we can see ourselves in the right way: a human being that made a mistake. It's highly unlikely that this is the first mistake you ever made and it's not the last mistake you will ever make. We are not perfect in our actions, thoughts, words, or deeds - though it is good that we should strive to be perfect (Genesis 17:1, Matthew 5:48). We are not perfect in our dealings with others, though God loves us regardless. We are not perfect in how we handle our recriminations, though God loves us even in our failures. We are perfectly loved by God. Remember, God does not love us because we are good, but because *He* is good (Romans 5:8).

Our humility lets us step down from the pedestal of perfections that our ego and cognitive biases try to set us upon. Our humility allows us to *accept* that we are imperfect and make mistakes, without our internal monologue launching into a vitriolic tirade about how horrible we are. Our humility allows us to seek God's forgiveness, and *accept* His forgiveness through the knowledge that His understanding is greater than our own. Our humility helps us understand the hurt or pain or difficulty we have caused the other person, and *accept* our responsibility for the actions that occurred through our own fallibility (Proverbs 28:13, Galatians 6:4-5).

Will there be consequences for our actions? Perhaps, and if there are, then that is something that we must bear because of our mistake. We must take ownership of our actions, but not let our actions take ownership of our soul. Being forgiven by God does not mean we are free from punishment or discipline here on Earth, but it does mean we are free of punishment for that sin on the day of reckoning.

Will others mistreat us for our actions? Perhaps, and if they do, we must call on our humility. When reproached by others for something we have done, we must remember that they, too, are imperfect beings with their own struggles. Whether or not you deserve their reproach, you must be forgiving of them as our Lord has instructed us to. Think of them and what they are feeling first, think of yourself afterwards. Acknowledge your fault, offer your heartfelt apology, and then forgive them. By forgiving them, you are lessening your own struggle with the fallout of your sin.

This can be a difficult thing to bear: the recriminations of others, the finger pointing, the whispers, the gossip, etc. Don't rise to their challenge! Don't lash out at them in self-defense, don't respond with a, "yeah, but ..." Don't let yourself be goaded into an argument that cannot prevail against their self-righteous indignation. Know that their mean-spirited comments and treatments are doing nothing to heal the situation; they are only giving in to their anger (fear) and dealing with it in a way that is as injurious to them, as it may be to you.

> *"I remember my affliction and my wandering, the bitterness and the gall. I well remember them, and my soul is downcast within me. Yet this I call to mind and therefore I have hope: Because of the Lord's great love we are not consumed, for his compassions never fail. They are new every morning; great is your faithfulness. I say to myself, "The Lord is my portion; therefore I will wait for him."* (Lamentations 3:19-24)

This passage from Jeremiah, in the book of Lamentations, tells us how at the worst of times, he was able to pull himself up and keep going because of God's love for him. As Pastor Chuck Smith explains:[156]

> "Jeremiah was at one of the lowest points of his life. There is a dramatic change as Jeremiah adjusts his thinking. We can think ourselves into hopelessness and despair, or by the renewing of our mind we can come into a whole new state of consciousness of God to attain victory and hope. The fact that I wake up each morning is proof of God's mercy, compassion, and faithfulness. The Lord is all I need."

In chapter five I quoted Matthew Henry's *Commentary on Ephesians 4*[75]. One of the things this commentary explained about the dangers of sinful anger was:

> "Neither give place to the calumniator, or the false accuser" (so some read the words); that is, "let your ears be deaf to whisperers, talebearers, and slanderers."

Remember that as you walk through those tribulations, walk rightly (i.e.: forgivingly, humbly) and know that you do not walk alone.

> *"The Lord is my light and my salvation—whom shall I fear? The Lord is the stronghold of my life—of whom shall I be afraid? When the wicked advance against me to devour me, it is my enemies and my foes who will stumble and fall. Though an army besiege me, my heart will not fear; though war break out against me, even then I will be confident." (Psalm 27:1-3)*

> *"Have I not commanded you? Be strong and courageous. Do not be afraid; do not be discouraged, for the Lord your God will be with you wherever you go." (Joshua 1:9)*

Marriage and Family Therapist, Doug Britton, explains the benefit of humility when faced with failure and reproach:[157]

> <u>You can eat "humble pie" without being crushed when you are humble.</u>
>
> When you are humble, you can respond to and learn from criticism without becoming defensive—whether it is deserved or not deserved. Likewise, you can be aware of your failures without being emotionally devastated.

God's forgiveness is not a free ticket

I had the argument put to me by a friend that if we sin and then are forgiven by God, why can't we continue to act sinfully, knowing that each time God will forgive us?

We have to look at this through two different lenses of understanding. The first lens is that of the confession of Paul, the man whose writings form a significant portion of the New Testament. In Romans 7, he talks about *habitual sin* and his personal struggle with it:

> *"I do not understand what I do. For what I want to do I do not do, but what I hate I do." (Romans 7:15)*

> *"For I do not do the good I want to do, but the evil I do not want to do—this I keep on doing." (Romans 7:19)*

Through the reading of Romans chapter seven, we learn how Paul understood that there was sin in him and that he could not change that sinful nature on his own. In chapter eight, Paul goes on to talk about the redemptive power of the Holy Spirit, and the desire of a person to live in accordance with the spirit, rather than living according to the flesh (Romans 8:4).

Before I gave my life to God, accepting his love and forgiveness for my sins, I lived in accordance with the desires of the flesh. The person that I was back then engaged in blasphemy, that is, taking God's name or Jesus' name in vain, and I did it frequently. It was to the point that a woman at work had to take me aside and ask me to stop because it bothered her. When I gave my life to God, I became very aware of those things I was saying. One of the first things I wanted to change about myself in that new life was to stop swearing (blaspheming).

It happened, but it didn't happen overnight. My mannerisms and patterns of speech were deeply seated in how my mind responded to things. Coming out with — you can imagine the things I said — were, seemingly, second nature. It took time for me to change this. Today, I can't remember the last time that I took Their names in vain. I have reconditioned my mind to say things like, "for goodness sake."

As I worked to change my ways, when I slipped up and blasphemed, I confessed it to God and asked for forgiveness; renewing my promise to myself to continue my pursuit of change. Eventually, I was able to break this *habitual sin* and put it behind me. This is only one example, though, of habitual sin.

Relevant Magazine published an article about habitual sin by Jed Brewer, director of productions for Mission USA:[158]

> The main thing that our well-meaning brothers and sisters are confused about, though, is the nature of God's forgiveness. The truth is, it just doesn't run out.
>
> Jesus said if your brother wrongs you the same way seven times in a single day, you should forgive him (Luke 17:4). Further, you should be prepared to forgive the same person 70 times seven times (Matthew 18:22). And the Bible tells us our forgiveness of others is to mirror God's forgiveness of us (Ephesians 4:32).
>
> What all this means is that God has an impossibly high ability to forgive us. Which is good, because we have an impossibly high ability to sin. And isn't that exactly what the Bible says? "Where sin increased, grace increased all the more" (Romans 5:20).

When we choose to believe in Christ (follow his example), we are choosing to change our life. While we know we have a sinful nature, our desire to be close to God and to live as Jesus teaches us will cause us, if we are sincere in our desire, to want to behave better. We must pursue the changes in our lives to bring us in line with His teachings. However, by our nature, we are sinful, we are not perfect, and we make mistakes.

In Mathew 18:22, Jesus tells us to forgive, *"not seven times, but seventy-seven times."* This means that our forgiveness of others is to be unending. If that is how forgiving we are supposed to be, then how much greater is the capacity of God to forgive? As you work to change the habitual sins in your life, the sins that you default to, know that God is still with you, still forgiving you, and you should focus on your successes rather than your failures as you continue to try to change your ways.

But what if it is not a habitual sin? What if you *want to sin* because it feels good?

The Bible contains a very clear and definitive answer to that question, found in Hebrews 7:26-31:

> *If we deliberately keep on sinning after we have received the knowledge of the truth, no sacrifice for sins is left, but only a fearful expectation of judgment and of raging fire that will consume the enemies of God. Anyone who rejected the law of Moses died without mercy on the testimony of two or three witnesses. How much more severely do you think someone deserves to be punished who has trampled the Son of God underfoot, who has treated as an unholy thing the blood of the covenant that sanctified them, and who has insulted the Spirit of grace? For we know him who said, "It is mine to avenge; I will repay," and again, "The Lord will judge his people." It is a dreadful thing to fall into the hands of the living God.*

When we make the conscious decision to sin, knowing full well that it is against God's law or the teachings of Jesus, then we have *"trampled the Son of God underfoot."* In a more modern turn of phrase, *we have spit in Jesus' face.*

The inspired word of God is very clear that, while the blood of the Lamb has washed away your sin, if you *deliberately keep on sinning* then *no sacrifice for sins is left.* In other words, if you make the decision to do something for fun, or that feels good, and *you know* it is a sin, then there is no forgiveness for it. This is a much more pointed reiteration of an antecedent we find in the Old Testament book of Habakkuk 2:4:

> *"See, the enemy is puffed up; his desires are not upright — but the righteous person will live by his faithfulness —"*

When we make the conscious decision to sin, knowing it is against God's law, we are not living by our faithfulness, we are living in the realm of the flesh (Romans 7:5).

> *"Enter through the narrow gate. For wide is the gate and broad is the road that leads to destruction, and many enter through it. But small is the gate and narrow the road that leads to life, and only a few find it." (Matthew 7:13-14)*

Because we desire to walk through the narrow gate, we strive to walk through life following the teachings we have been given. If you are trying to walk in a just manner, but trip up, God will pick you up, dust you off, and let you keep walking. His merciful spirit rejoices in your desire and attempts to change. His forgiveness is always there for you, as are His compassion and understanding.

However, when you make a choice to act contrary to his law, when you make the death of Jesus meaningless through your rejection of the redemption that he offers you (because refusing to believe in him, that means to follow him, is rejection), then why would you expect there to be no cost for your actions?

If you are making the decision to sin, then there is no free ticket.

Forgiveness does not come from a vending machine; it comes from a committed relationship between two: you and God. Keep up your part of the commitment!

Summary

Not being able to let go (what psychologists call not being able to achieve self-forgiveness), often leads to depression, especially in older adults.[159]

One of the most stirring passages in the Bible about finding respite in God's forgiveness is Psalm 32. In this passage, David is writing about how he felt while he wallowed in the misery of his shame, and how he emerged from that misery into peace when he truthfully confessed his sin to God with the full humility resulting from his guilt. From this, we need to take the lesson that no matter how we beat ourselves up, or in the words of David, *"through my groaning all day long,"* we can rely on the compassion and love of God to heal us, *if we fully place our love and trust in Him*:

> *Blessed is the one whose transgressions are forgiven, whose sins are covered.*
>
> *Blessed is the one whose sin the Lord does not count against them and in whose spirit is no deceit.*
>
> *When I kept silent, my bones wasted away through my groaning all day long.*
>
> *For day and night your hand was heavy on me; my strength was sapped as in the heat of summer.*

Then I acknowledged my sin to you and did not cover up my iniquity. I said, "I will confess my transgressions to the Lord." And you forgave the guilt of my sin.

Therefore let all the faithful pray to you while you may be found; surely the rising of the mighty waters will not reach them.

You are my hiding place; you will protect me from trouble and surround me with songs of deliverance.

I will instruct you and teach you in the way you should go; I will counsel you with my loving eye on you.

Do not be like the horse or the mule, which have no understanding but must be controlled by bit and bridle or they will not come to you.

Many are the woes of the wicked, but the Lord's unfailing love surrounds the one who trusts in him.

Rejoice in the Lord and be glad, you righteous; sing, all you who are upright in heart!

Chapter 11

The Unforgiven

"Cries for justice are often the bitter laments of the vengeful." — Wayne Gerard Trotman

Dealing with being unforgiven by another person can be a crushing weight to bear, whether our action that hurt them was an offence of omission or commission, accidental or careless, reactionary or thoughtless.

In chapter eight I wrote about empathy, and in chapter nine I wrote about changing your perspective. As much as these are necessary to give forgiveness, empathy and perspective are also important in understanding a lack of forgiveness from another person.

You have hurt someone, and you have *accepted* that. You are responsible for your actions, no one else is, and you have *accepted* that. Whatever the offence, you own the guilt for it, and you have *accepted* that. Perhaps the forgiveness from that person is something that they are working on, but they just haven't gotten there yet. You need to *accept* that it may take a long time for them to be able to forgive you. You may also need to *accept* that the relationship has been permanently damaged, or forever changed in a way that you don't want.

Have you asked for forgiveness (confessed)?

This can be an incredibly hard thing to do in some situations, but it is still a vital part of the process of healing. When we ask another for forgiveness, we are confessing our actions to them. We are acknowledging our fault and *accepting* responsibility for what we have done, directly to the person that the action affected.

The unfortunate aspect of asking for forgiveness is that when the person gives their forgiveness, they may not be doing so genuinely. This is not due to any deception on their part. They may say you are forgiven to keep the peace, but in their heart, they still harbour resentment. They may want to be forgiving, but not really know *how* to be forgiving. Then we will find that our transgression against them comes up at the oddest times, even during arguments about completely unrelated matters. Though they will tell us we have been forgiven, they become hypersensitive to things you say and do, because their attachment to that past hurt is still strong.

Regardless, the act of asking for forgiveness is a part of the healing process. Just like a sin against God, where we confess and repent, we must also follow that same guideline with our victim. The confession of what you did is just as important to them. They need the acknowledgement that you know you did wrong, and that you have *accepted* your role in their hurt.

> *"Therefore, if you are offering your gift at the altar and there remember that your brother or sister has something against you, leave your gift there in front of the altar. First go and be reconciled to them; then come and offer your gift." (Matthew 5:23-24)*

Repentance

They need to know that you are repentant. Simply saying, "Sorry," isn't enough. That overused expression tends to mean very little for many people. Some of us are conditioned to say, "I'm sorry," and in response, "It's okay," from early childhood. That exchange of phrases, for some, becomes rote and meaningless. However, when you demonstrate a true understanding of what you did wrong, articulating your transgression, and then articulate your repentance, the conversation can be much more healing and restorative.

Tell them how you see that you have hurt them, and the regret that you carry for that. Acknowledge that your actions were unfair, inappropriate, or just plain thoughtless. Let them know that you *accept* responsibility for the actions which have led them to feeling hurt, and let them know you are open to hearing what you can do to help the healing, to help them.

It is vitally important that you be open and truthful in your apology and demonstrate your understanding of your offence.

> *"Therefore, having put away falsehood, let each one of you speak the truth with his neighbor, for we are members one of another." (Ephesians 4:25)*

Restitution

Perhaps your offence was such that they suffered a pecuniary or property loss. With your confession and repentance, don't forget to offer restitution. When you do offer restitution, don't limit yourself to a pound for a pound, offer further restitution (by act, word, deed, or valuable consideration) to demonstrate your true repentance, much as Zacchaeus did:

> *Jesus entered Jericho and was passing through. A man was there by the name of Zacchaeus; he was a chief tax collector and was wealthy. He wanted to see who Jesus was, but because he was short he could not see over the crowd. So he ran ahead and climbed a sycamore-fig tree to see him, since Jesus was coming that way. When Jesus reached the spot, he looked up and said to him, "Zacchaeus, come down immediately. I must stay at your house today." So he came down at once and welcomed him gladly. All the people saw this and began to mutter, "He has gone to be the guest of a sinner." But Zacchaeus stood up and said to the Lord, "Look, Lord! Here and now I give half of my possessions to the poor, and if I have cheated anybody out of anything, I will pay back four times the amount." Jesus said to him, "Today salvation has come to this house, because this man, too, is a son of Abraham. For the Son of Man came to seek and to save the lost." (Luke 19:1-10)*

It's more about them than it is about you

The absence of forgiveness is not about the Unforgiven; it's about the unforgiving. Whether or not a person can forgive depends on many factors: how deeply they were hurt, the effect of that hurt, their desire to be forgiving in general, whether they can provide unconditional forgiveness or only conditional forgiveness, the history between victim and perpetrator, etc.

If a person refuses to forgive you, then you need to rely on the forgiveness from God for your sin as being sufficient for you to move on. Through the unforgiveness of another, you may have lost a friend, damaged a relationship, or caused a rift in your family.

You need to *accept* that this has happened and move forward. You need to *accept* that there is nothing else you can do to repent to another person.

I know there are things in my past that I have not been forgiven for. I don't consider for one second that this is okay, because someone out there may still be hurting from things that happened decades ago, or maybe they have managed to let go of it and have healed. I don't know, as I don't have any contact with them anymore. I regret my actions, I regret that I hurt them, and I regret that I do not have the opportunity to offer amends of any kind. That is a regret that I carry, but it does not eat me up (anymore). For the things that I did in my past, I've made myself right with God. Even though I know that I am forgiven by Him and that I still regret my past actions, I know that I cannot hold on to them and have them control my life, so I have *accepted* them and moved forward. I also remember those things as opportunities for me to learn about myself, see myself through eyes of humility, and change how I behave (for the good) in the future.

> *God does not want you to go through the rest of your life punishing yourself for your sins. Jesus said to a woman who had lived an immoral lifestyle, "Your sins are forgiven. Your faith has saved you; go in peace" (Luke 7:47-50).*

The absentee victim

It can be exacerbated when the victim of our misdeed is no longer available to us to seek forgiveness from. Perhaps they have moved, passed away, or simply refuse to communicate with you. Regardless of why your victim is unavailable, you still need to process your *accepted* guilt. Whether the victim is deceased, unavailable, or refuses to communicate with you, you need to understand chapter 10, how we *accept* our own guilt.

Chapter 12

Incredible Acts of Forgiveness

Forgiveness may be needed for the person that swipes your purse, steals your laptop, hits their car with your car, or takes the last piece of apple pie that you were saving for your tea. On the other extreme, you may be challenged to find forgiveness for the person that killed your child while they were driving drunk, the person that shot your spouse during a robbery, or the family member that abused you in unseemly ways for many years.

While I've never had to forgive a person, in-person, for horrible acts, I have had to forgive the memory of a person. It's hard for a man to admit that they've been the victim of sexual impropriety, but some of us have. As an adult, I never had the opportunity to face the first person from my childhood, but I did eventually come to understand them and have given forgiveness posthumously.

As an adult, the second person from my childhood, I chose to be forgiving without addressing it with them, because to do so would have destroyed them. I had a relationship with that person all of my life, and I had come to understand the weakness they were suffering when their *attempt* occurred. I was able to let go of that hurt, let go of that past, and move forward with my life.

For the third person, from something that happened when I was an adult, I held on to hatred for a long, long time. It was only through the processes in this book that I was able to finally come to a place of forgiveness for them. I have no contact with them and don't even know if they are still alive, nor do I care to make contact with them if they are alive. The hatred I used to feel for them, however, is gone. I had to look at my anger, understand the fear, peel away the emotional onion, and then try to see the situation from a broader perspective; taking into account many lessons I've learned over the years. It is difficult, but it *can* be done. The forgiveness for them, for what they did, is there for them.

Whatever the reasons are that you are exploring the concept of forgiveness, you need to know that there are others who have made surprising and incredible steps forward in the ability to forgive. My research has introduced me to some incredible and moving stories of forgiveness, in a variety of situations, which I want to share with you.

Eva Mozes Kor[160]

For close to forty years, Holocaust survivor Eva Mozes Kor has preached the controversial message of forgiveness. When asked about forgiving and forgetting, she is very firm in her answer in this article from *The Times of Israel*:

> "That is a slogan that has no merit in its facts, because how on earth could anybody forget their whole family was murdered. That's stupid. People remember, but the way you remember and why you remember should be different," said Kor, rolling her r's with a rich Hungarian accent despite her 60 years as an American.

> "Not because you want to get even with them, you remember because this is part of your life, and you are, each person is, a product of their past. So how can I forget my past?" asked Kor.

The crux of the controversy is a well-publicized 1995 proclamation declaring her across-the-board forgiveness of the Nazis. For this she is reviled by many, if not most, of her fellow Holocaust survivors and their offspring. She said she is derided for what they label a cheap publicity stunt and horrific overstepping of boundaries.

For her part, she too is no placid Buddha: In our conversation, she railed against the rabbinic establishment for its inability to adopt her perspective to heal the Jewish peoplehood, and cited the German courts' "stupidity."

For over 20 years, Kor has stood up to the wrath of her peers and continued to endorse the healing power of forgiveness as the one true path to shedding victimization. Reclaiming her personal power, said Kor, is her "ultimate revenge" against the Nazis.

So, why would a person who has lost so much be willing or even able to forgive? An excellent answer to this question comes from Sammy Rangel, a man who has had a great deal to forgive, and to be forgiven for.

Sammy Rangel[161]

In a TEDx talk titled The Power of Forgiveness, Sammy Rangel gives this explanation at the end of the talk:

> "What I have learned, is that although the details of our lives may be different, the underlying process of getting stuck in our suffering is the same for all of us. We do not have to be victims of our experiences or in the way we tell our stories, but interestingly enough, stories are the only way out, and it is us who creates those stories. We hold the

power to change our stories, and what they represent. Create the new story and new path, the things that one day held you down, will hold you up."

Colleen Haggerty[162]

Colleen Haggerty, who lost her leg in a car accident where someone crossed the line, has found forgiveness, but it didn't come quickly. It didn't come until years later when she got to speak to the man that took her leg. Where she had only known her own pain, grief, discomfort, difficulties, and challenges, she had never known about his side of the experience. She knew going to meet him that she wanted to yell and scream and beat him on the chest, but she didn't: instead, she listened.

She learned how the accident had impacted him, and all that he had been through because of it. She said that day she, "met Harvey, and met my compassionate self." She said that when she forgave him, she felt *empowered*. The bitter feelings that still come up no longer reminder her that she is a victim, instead, they remind her to be forgiving. She tells how when she could forgive the past, she could create the future she wanted, and that each time she forgives, she opens the door onto the possibility of whom she could be.

She closes her talk by saying, "The choice to forgive is always a gift we give ourselves."

Rachel King[163]

Part of Rachel King's moving talk about forgiveness is when, at the age of 14, she was sexually abused by a member of the church congregation she belonged to.

She tells how it turned her world upside down and the fact that faith was thrown into it made it worse. It's been a long and hard journey for her to be able to say she forgives her perpetrator. She tells the audience that she understands that, "forgiveness is letting go of all hope for the past, and using your story to move forward and inspire others; to send forth that message of hope."

Dr. Chuck Sandstrom[164]

In June 2009, Dr. Chuck Sandstrom was brutally attacked by a drunk, angry man. He punched Dr. Sandstrom, and his head hit a brick wall behind him. Close to death, unconscious for almost six weeks, he suffered a severe traumatic brain injury. He lost his job and his home. His free-spirited wife became his twenty-four-hour caregiver. He says, "the surprising thing about the assault that ended our lives, is that we lived through it!"

However, he talks very openly about forgiving the man that assaulted him. While they claim to be nothing special, they have learned that forgiveness can take ordinary people on an extraordinary journey. The slow and difficult journey broke their hearts wide open with their need for God and one another. They were able to see the assailant and his family's lives were changed almost overnight. The assailant was hiding from U.S. Marshals who would have shot him on sight, yet he was still taking great risks to see his small children. He quotes Rabbi Harold Kushner in saying that, "Forgiveness is first and foremost, a way of seeing. It cannot change the facts of the world we live in, but it can change the way we see the facts."

While most see Dr. Sandstrom's injury as a tragedy, they have come to see it as a way to love more deeply. The couple doesn't take being alive and being able to love for granted, and it's an attitude they sustain each day.

When the man who assaulted Dr. Sandstrom was sentenced, the sentencing did not bring healing. What helped them most was reaching out to that man's family and helping them stand up again. When the man learned of Dr. Sandstrom's forgiveness, he said to his wife that he had never felt loved like he did at that moment.

Anne-Marie Cockburn[165]

In July 2013, Anne-Marie Cockburn lost her 15-year-old daughter to half a gramme of ecstasy. It was sold to her by a 17-year-old boy who went to jail for it. Anne-Marie has chosen to continue living, rather than let her life die with that of her child. She says:

> "I haven't felt angry as I've converted my anger into positive action. Allowing anger to fester would be the final nail in the coffin for me. I have looked for positive and healthy ways to cope because if I don't find ways to be happy in my new life I will not survive. I have never focussed much on the offender because I don't need retribution. What he did was very unfortunate but he didn't do it deliberately. At the final hearing I said that I didn't want him to go to prison, although some of my family disagree with me. They wanted him to be punished but I just said, "I'll never ever get justice for Martha because she's dead so why waste two young lives instead of just one". I hope he does something good with his life, something he can be proud of."

Christopher Emmanuel[166]

As a child growing up in a small town in Grenada, West Indies, Christopher Emmanuel was mercilessly shamed in front of his peers by his father. As a result, he buried the anger until it erupted in mental illness several years later. After 10 years in and out of institutions, he was able to heal and forgive his father. Now as a counsellor, he lives in Toronto and teaches the power of forgiveness. Christopher says:

> "Forgiveness took away the illusion that my past had made me powerless. It rekindled my faith in a higher power, strengthened my sense of morality, and created a totally new reality."

Margot Van Sluytman[167]

From the Forgiveness Project comes an eye-opening story of forgiveness:

> When Margot Van Sluytman was 8-years-old her parents moved from Guyana to Canada in order to bring up their three children in a safer environment. In March 1978, when she was 16, Margot's father was murdered during an armed robbery at the Hudson Bay store where he worked. Many years later Margot embarked on a path of reconciliation with her father's killer. Today she is a poet, publisher and founder of the Sawbonna Project (sawbonna.wordpress.com), a justice organisation that encourages respect, responsibility, and relationship within the crucible of our shared-humanity.
>
> Her story continues by telling us that "It turned out that Glen Flett (who had transformed his life in prison and been

released after 14 years of incarceration) had attended an event aiming to bring victims and perpetrators together, where a woman had asked if he ever thought about contacting the family of his victim. When he replied 'yes', she went away to research what I was doing and then showed him my publishing press work.

So I replied to Glen's wife to thank her for the donation and ask if her husband would consider giving me an apology. She emailed straight back saying, 'he has been waiting a long time to do this.'

From then on Glen and I started to exchange emails. They were emails filled with humanity. His words helped to heal me, but after a while the words weren't enough and I knew I needed to look into his eyes. So three months later I met the man who killed my father …

At first I hated the very notion of forgiveness. To tell someone who is in pain to forgive is brutal. Forgiveness can't be prescriptive. But at a talk one day an audience member told me she had chosen to forgive the perpetrator of a heinous crime and this made me wonder if perhaps I was being too narrow minded. The moment I began to consider forgiveness, my whole body started to feel different, more complete and more at peace.

For me forgiveness is a fluid process which means healing. Before I embarked on this path half of me was a void and full of nothingness, whereas now I have a friendship with the man who killed my father and that has helped put meaning back into my life."

You can read more about Margot's project here: http://sawbonna.blogspot.ca

Katy Hutchison[168,169]

On New Year's Eve 1997, Katy Hutchison's husband, Bob, was beaten to death while checking on a party being thrown by his neighbour's son. In the small town of Squamish in British Columbia, a wall of silence soon grew up around the murder. She tells her story of incredible forgiveness:

> Eventually, after four years, Ryan Aldridge was arrested. That same day, as I was leaving the police station, I spotted him on camera, alone in the investigation room. The police had left the tape rolling and I stood and watched him falling apart. I didn't want to leave him.
>
> After his arrest, police officers showed Ryan a video I'd made for him urging him to dig down deep to find the words to say, "I did this". Four years of silence, grief and fear then fell away as he fulfilled my wish and confessed to the crime. Those words would begin the healing process for both of us. He then stunned police by asking to meet me, and so, less than 24 hours after his arrest, I found myself face-to-face with the man who had murdered my husband. As he sobbed it was all I could do not to hold him. Second to the day I gave birth, it was probably the most human moment of my life.
>
> Some time into Ryan's sentence I discovered an incredible organization called Community Justice Initiatives that was able to organize a Victim-Offender Reconciliation between Ryan and I. It took place in the prison and lasted most of the day: we spoke about almost everything – our lives, our hobbies, our families. There were tears there were long

silences where neither of us had the words to fill the space. In that meeting I told Ryan that I had forgiven him.

I've been able to forgive Ryan because of the immense sympathy I have for his mother. I understood her loss. We haven't met yet but we write and I cherish her letters. Forgiveness isn't easy. Taking tranquillizers and having someone look after your kids would probably be easier, but I feel compelled to do something with Bob's legacy. I want to tell my story to help change people's perceptions – and where possible I want to do this with Ryan by my side. I'll never understand how our universes collided – but they did, and as Bob can't make further contribution to society, then perhaps Ryan can. Whether victim or perpetrator, part of being human is rolling up our sleeves and taking an active part in repairing harm.

Amelia and Sam have fully supported my choice to forgive Ryan, but others have asked, "How could you?" The way I saw it how could I not? My children had lost their father and I did not want them to lose me in the process. If I had been consumed by hatred, anger and vengeance, what kind of mother would I be? Something happened when Bob died and I found my voice. Forgiveness became an opportunity to create a new and hopeful beginning.

Looking back 17 years, I realize how dynamic the forgiveness experience has been. It changes shape; some days growing, others withering. It is heart work of the highest order. I am thankful to Ryan for making the very best of his life, moving forward and working hard to care for his family and contribute to his community. But mostly I remain grateful for the brave hearts of my now-adult children and my second husband Michael, who supported my choice and trusted me on this uncharted journey of the heart.

Ryan has since been released from prison. He is employed and happily married with one child. Katy has since written the book *Walking After Midnight: One Woman's Journey Through Murder, Justice, and Forgiveness.* For further information you can visit Katy's website www.katyhutchisonpresents.com.

Wayne Braden[170]

In May, 2009, Valereen Kaleohano-Knittle was sentenced to ten years in prison for a DUI that ended with the death of a 17-month-old little girl, Aliyah Braden, and the critical injury of her mother. From the below-cited article in *Hawaii News Now*, we read:

> "I stand before you today with my head down in shame and with guilt for what I have taken from you," Kaleohano-Knittle said through tears. "You may never be able to forgive me. I have deprived you of your child."
>
> The defendant pleaded guilty to first-degree negligent homicide, first-degree negligent injury, consuming or possessing intoxicating liquor while operating a motor vehicle, and inattention to driving.
>
> Prosecutors say beer and a bottle of Jack Daniel's were found in her pickup.
>
> "I acknowledge the devastation that I have caused in your life," Kaleohano-Knittle said. "Your continuing pain and sorrow are in my heart forever."

The 51-year-old says she no longer drinks, attends Alcoholics Anonymous meetings, and wants to speak about her experience to schools and community groups.

"I will work tirelessly to keep drunk drivers off the road," she said through tears. "I'm sorry. I'm so sorry."

Wayne Braden then stood up and hugged his daughter's killer, bringing others in the courtroom to tears.

"What I just witnessed was one of the most extraordinary acts of compassion and contrition that I have seen," Elizabeth Strance, Circuit Court judge, said.

When asked about this later, Wayne Braden, Aliyah's father, said that he, "believed she was a decent woman who made a terrible mistake."

Ady Guzman-DeJesus[171,172]

An article in the U.K. Daily Mail tells about Jordyn Howe, 15, who brought his step-father's gun to school and accidentally shot, and killed, his 13-year-old friend Lourdes 'Jina' Guzman-DeJesus. Through a plea deal, he saw no jail time, but attended vocational training at Park Youth Academy for a year. Still, Lourdes' mother Ady decided to forgive Howe in the courtroom during his sentence:

> Struggling through her tears, Ady Guzman-DeJesus walked towards 16-year-old Jordyn Howe in a Miami court on Tuesday, put her arms around him and held him tightly.
>
> 'Justice is done,' Guzman-DeJesus told reporters outside the courtroom. 'I miss her and I really do forgive him.'

Jordyn now speaks publicly about the dangers of guns, alongside his victim's mother.

Jordan Byelich[173,174]

In September 2014, Mitzi Nelson was texting behind the wheel of her car when she struck and killed cyclist Jill Byelich. After she was sentenced, the victim's husband, Jordan Byelich, approached her, hugged her, and said, "I'll pray for you." He later told a Fox News reporter that it was compassion his wife would have shown, always looking for the silver lining.

Nelson's lawyer said that gesture will stick with her, and start the long process of writing a wrong. As part of her probation, she has to talk to 20 driver's education classes about the dangers of texting while driving. Jordan told a Fox News reporter, "I hope that out of this there's a learning opportunity where she can pass on some of the things she went through and maybe it will prevent something else in the future."

Sandra Walker[175]

In November 2011, 35-year-old Glen Walker and 16-year-old Joshua Jenkins were killed in a car accident. Joshua Jenkins was in the car driven by Tamara Matthews, his mother, when it slammed into the Walker family car. She had drifted over the centre line on the road. Charged with homicide by vehicle and failure to maintain lane, after she pled guilty she spoke with Sandra Walker who lost her husband that day. They hugged, as Sandra told Tamara that she forgave her. Sandra Walker later said, "I know she is going through as much pain as I am feeling. I wanted her to know that I forgive her for what she did."

Renée Napier[176]

Impaired driver, Eric Smallridge, killed Meagan Napier and her friend, Lisa Dickson, in 2002. Before his sentencing, he wrote a letter of apology to Renée, Meagan's mother, and then apologised to her again in court. A few years later, Renée asked a judge to reduce Eric's 22-year sentence by half, and the judge obliged.

An article on *CBS News'* website tells us:

> Renee's 180-degree shift began with the single turn of a single phrase. First at Eric's sentencing and later in a letter, Renee told Eric she'd forgiven him, even though, at the time, she hadn't -- not really. At trial, Eric had actually been pretty defensive and unapologetic.
>
> "I could hate him forever and the world would tell me that I have a right to do that," Renee says. "It's not going to do me any good, and it's not going to do him any good. I would grow old and bitter and angry and hateful. ... In my opinion, forgiveness is the only way to heal."
>
> She says it did heal her -- almost as much as it healed him.
>
> "It was like a burden," he says. "It was a weight off my chest. I no longer had to hide behind this facade."
>
> Following the forgiveness, Eric apologized repeatedly and profusely -- in private and in public -- to the families of both girls. Eventually, Lisa's parents forgave him, too, which only inspired Eric to atone even more.

While in prison, with the assistance of the prison bureau, Eric began attending presentations to schools with Renée to talk about the dangers of impaired driving. Upon his release, they have continued this practice.

After his sentencing, Renée wrote an opinion for the *Pensacola News & Journal*. In it, she says[177]:

> "... the only thing I can hope for is that I am living my life to the fullest and that my life glorifies God. Grief is like a black cloud that drops down on us and its as though it has a vacuum that sucks the life right out of you. I instantly felt as though nothing in life is really important and things I stressed are trivial. We should place a value on other people in our lives and our relationships ...
>
> ... all my life I have prayed for God to help me be forgiving and sometimes forgiveness comes easy and sometimes it is the most difficult thing to do. My experience has taught me that once we forgive those who have hurt us healing begins, it frees us so that we can move forward unencumbered."

Davey Blackburn[178,179]

Davey and his wife Amanda planted the Resonate Church (Indianapolis, IN) in 2012. On November 10th, 2015, while Davey was at the gym for a workout, his wife was viciously beaten and shot three times. When asked about his forgiveness for the two men that did this, Davey said in both of the cited articles:

> "I don't want to live my life going down the path of bitterness because it will destroy my soul and it will destroy

everybody around me if I choose that (unforgiveness)," explained Blackburn.

"So today, I choose forgiveness. And tomorrow, I pray that I can wake up and choose forgiveness by the power of Jesus Christ. One of the things about Jesus when they were inflicting way more pain than any of us can imagine on Him, on the cross, He looked out and he said, 'Father, forgive them, for they don't know what they're doing.' And so that spirit lives in us and we're just praying His spirit would help us in that," he added.

Mary Johnson[180]

Mary's son, Laramiun Byrd, was shot to death at a party in 1993 by Oshea Israel. At his sentencing, Mary hugged Oshea and told him that she forgave him. Afterwards, she was in shock at what she had done. But then, as reported in the cited article on TODAY.com:

> It was then, Johnson recalls, that she was set free. "I felt something leave me," she said. "Instantly I knew all the hatred, bitterness and animosity — I knew it was gone."

The article on Mary Johnson's forgiveness goes on to speak about such acts in such horrible circumstances, quoting the director of the Stanford University's Forgiveness Project:

> While Johnson's experience sounds extraordinary, experts say that forgiveness of this magnitude is more possible that one might imagine — though Dr. Fred Luskin, a psychologist and director of the Stanford University Forgiveness Project, says coming to this stage very quickly is less common.

Those who let go of intense anger immediately after a tragic loss, he said, may have long practiced a forgiving attitude, which can "hard wire" the behavior so that it becomes like a reflex. It's also possible that forgiveness can be premature, a gesture that protects someone from the "absolute horror" of what happened. Finally, Luskin said, some people experience early forgiveness as a form of grace. "In the midst of unimagined pain, something comes in and gives you a way out to peacefulness," he told TODAY.com.

Kate & Andy Grosmaire[181]

In March 2010, Kate and Andy learned that their youngest daughter, 19-year-old Ann, had been shot by her boyfriend and fiancé, Conor McBride. After a few days of arguing, Conor had put a loaded shotgun under his chin, but then stopped as Ann entered the house. As the argument resumed, he pointed the gun at her and pulled the trigger, shooting her through the eye. Ann didn't die immediately, but she never regained consciousness either. Five days later, Kate and Andy made the decision to remove life support.

Ann's parents had known Conor, an honour student in a leadership program, for quite a while. After he had killed their daughter, both Kate and Andy were able to forgive Conor. In the cited article on the *Good Housekeeping* website, Kate said:

> No one ever fully recovers from the death of a child. But I wanted to be someone who was happy and not hiding from the world, bitter and angry. Forgiveness was the way to peace — and I knew I would need that.

At first, Kate wanted Conor to serve the full 40 years-to-life that would be his sentence. However, after fourteen months, Andy regularly meeting with Conor's father (who was also losing a son through this), and the restorative justice process, Conor is serving 20 years with 10 years of probation. This is a sentence that Kate and Andy agreed to, as did Conor's parents. Kate's final words in the *Good Housekeeping* article are:

> My husband wanted answers. Through restorative justice, he got them. He doesn't have to worry that he could have done anything. He realized that there's nothing that he could have done.
>
> The power of forgiveness is not for the offender. It's for the person who is forgiving. When you can let go of that debt that's owed to you, there's a freedom and a peace on the other side.
>
> As Andy says, "We didn't have to go to jail with Conor." When someone is on death row, the family of their victims have been in jail too because they're tied to whether or not this man is executed or not. And I am so thankful that I don't have to live my life that way.

Chapter 13

The Framework of Forgiveness

We've covered a lot of ground on the topic of forgiveness. Now it's time to pull it together so that we can work from anger to forgiveness in a practical way.

Step 1 - Recognition

Recognise that you are angry. Depending on the intensity of your emotion, you may apply other labels to the feeling. Some words that come to mind are: bothered, ticked, upset, disturbed, mad, pissed off, *really* pissed off, incensed, apoplectic with … *you get the idea.* You need to recognise that you are angry, or dealing with emotion on the negative side of neutral, to recognise that you need to start with the remainder of the steps.

Step 2 - The 20-ish Minute Rule

No matter what the impetus is for your anger, remember that it takes time for your body to physiologically shake off the after effects of anger, even though the anger-pique itself only lasts a few seconds. How long it takes you to get back to a rational and reasoning state of mind will be different for each person. This is part of the importance of the chapter on knowing yourself.

If you have anxiety, then you tend to catastrophize situations[182,183,184] and believe them to be more onerous than they are. You may also have been affronted by more than one person, and need time to work out the actual "who said what" in your mind.

Regardless, a knee-jerk reaction to your anger is always a bad idea. Give yourself time to be rational, thoughtful, and work through the steps to understand your anger. Remember that time and distance helps us see things rationally, and give us time to think things through carefully.

Step 3 - Peel the Emotional Onion

Once you have settled down from the physiological response to your anger, start the work. Begin peeling back layer after layer of that emotional onion (or shuck the layers of the corn cob). Keep doing so until you can get to the root fear that lies behind your anger (or label of choice). Sometimes you will be able to do this quickly, other times it will take longer. Do the work — no one else is going to do it for you.

Step 4 - Take a Step Back - Change Your Perspective

When I was a child, suffering some unimaginable hurt by the words of another child, my mother never said: "stick and stones will break your bones, but names will never hurt me." She knew full well that names could hurt you. What she routinely did say, however, was that in 100 years, no one would know a thing about it.

The echo of her words has always reminded me to take a step back and look at a situation differently. I look at both sides of the affront. I look at my role and the other person's role. I look at the broader meaning of what transpired in terms of life, or work, or socialisation, depending on the situation. Then I start the process of changing my perspective and trying to see what transpired from that other person's frame of reference.

Step 5 - Get on Your Knees

By saying that, I mean that you should become fully engaged with your humility. It's good if you have someone *trusted* that you can talk to: friend, therapist, family member, pastor, etc. Talking the problem out loud helps. Putting your thoughts into articulated words may change how you see things, or how you think about things.

Revealing the fears deep inside us that provoke reactions can be a scary thing. However, putting primacy on how you appear to others is where the sin of pride will kick you hard, *very hard*. Notice those words "sin" and "pride"? What is the middle letter?

If we allow pride to prevent us from getting help, then it will take us longer to get to forgiveness, if we ever get there at all. In that situation, pride is interfering with your relationship with Jesus and with God.

"Rejoice in the Lord always. I will say it again: Rejoice! Let your gentleness be evident to all. The Lord is near. Do not be anxious about anything, but in every situation, by prayer and petition, with thanksgiving, present your

requests to God. And the peace of God, which transcends all understanding, will guard your hearts and your minds in Christ Jesus." (Philippians 4:4-7)

Don't forget to share your burden with God. He will hear you, and the Holy Spirit will respond. I have had amazing experiences where in a state of extreme frustration (anger), I have closed my eyes and shared that burden with God, reminding myself to place my burden in his loving hands and to trust in Him. I've never done this *without* a sense of calm and peace settling over me, which helped me see things more clearly and calmly.

Step 6 - The Past is Written, The Future is not.

Accept what transpired as being unchangeable. Then make the decision not to let the past grasp you with its grubby little fingers and hold you there. Decide to move forward, and away from the hurt. Speak to the person who affronted you if you care to, or don't. Remember that how you respond, and how much effect/damage that affront will have on you *is up to you*.

Step 7 - Forgive

Let go of the animosity towards the other person. Your ability to empathise, to change perspective, to look at the big picture, and to understand your own motivating fears will help you achieve this.

When you truly forgive, you no longer carry any desire for requital. You no longer have a need for revenge, or to see that person in a situation that is not beneficial to them. Forgiveness is an act of love, God's love acting through you. Don't dishonour that love by twisting it, lying to yourself or others about it, or letting pride demand that the wrong must be avenged.

Truly forgiving is freedom, it is an amazing thing you can do for yourself and for your relationship with God.

Chapter 14

Final Thoughts

There are some situations where forgiveness is easy, especially when you become more experienced at being forgiving. There are some situations where forgiveness will remain to be difficult, but not unattainable. Regardless of the amount of effort you have to put into it, forgiveness is a powerful way to let go of the hold that the past has on you.

Pragmatically speaking, forgiveness is not about what the other person needs; it is about how you intend to deal with the past. You can hold on to the hurt, the anger, and the bitterness. You can revel in it, roll around in it, wear it like a cloak, and present your pain and suffering as a badge of honour. But what does immersing yourself in that hurt and pain get you? It brings you a continuation of this hurt and pain. Yes, it's horrible that you had to endure whatever happened to you. It's unfair that someone purposefully or carelessly hurt you with the words that you heard. It's regrettable that you had to experience whatever the affront was. It's heartbreaking that you have had to shed so many tears. It's harrowing that you may have had to suffer through physical injuries and recovery challenges from an accident or physical assault.

But, how long do you plan on mentally and emotionally suffering? How long do you want to continue to re-experience the hurt? How many more precious minutes of life do you plan to spend in tears? How much control of your emotional health and mental health do you want to give to the past? How long do you wish to suffer?

The solution to the suffering that you put yourself through is forgiveness. You don't need anyone's permission to forgive. There are instances where people apply forgiveness against the advice of those who care for them. The One that cares for you most, however, *does* want you to apply forgiveness.

Forgiveness comes from love: not love for another person, but our love for God. He can fill our lives with a love that we need to share with others.

Do you feel it? Do you feel His love? Do you feel the peace and joy of the Holy Spirit moving within you? Is your relationship with God a surface relationship, or are you making it truly deep and meaningful? Do you *pisteuó*? The answers to these questions are between you and Him.

Whatever your level of relationship with God is, it cannot be clearer that He wants us to be forgiving. Forgiveness is one of the ways that we honour the sacrifice that Jesus made for us on the cross. Forgiveness is one of the teachings that we carry with us, and put into practice, in our belief (following) in Jesus. Forgiveness is one of the ways that God has given us to heal our hurts, and remove our suffering.

When you forgive, you may or may not help someone else heal, but you definitely put yourself on the healing path. Remember, *the absence of forgiveness is not about the Unforgiven, it's about the unforgiving.*

There is no downside to forgiveness, humility, or removing yourself from the grip of the past. Through forgiving, you change yourself: you let go of the hurt that continues to hurt you, you let go of the malice and hatred that darkens your heart, you stop the physical destruction of stress and anger, you can move forward in life by making the past powerless over you.

When you forgive, you transform the world you live in. When you forgive, you can transform others through your example. When you forgive, you can transform your relationship with God to make it deeper and more meaningful. Perhaps most importantly, when you forgive, you transform yourself.

"We must remember that the shortest distance between our problems and their solutions is the distance between our knees and the floor." — Charles F. Stanley

Discussion Questions

Presented here are some questions for discussion with your Christian study group, women's group, men's group, or perhaps with the family over dinner. As Christians, feel free to explore and question in your discussions, but remember that at the end of the day, it is the word of God in the Holy Bible that is our ultimate authority.

Question #1

One topic not covered in this book is "a humble vigilance over our own actions." What does this idea of humble vigilance mean to you, and how can you use it as a tool in both your interpersonal relationships and your relationship with God?

Question #2

In chapter seven I discussed the idea of "knowing yourself." In this, I presented a tool that I use where I stop periodically through the day to assess what has happened. Do you think this will be of benefit to you? Why do you think so? What other tools of self-reflection do you think you can use to better know yourself?

Question #3

Jesus has taught us to be forgiving in all things. Do you believe there is anything in your past that you cannot forgive another for? Perhaps you could discuss it with your group and get their perspective on the other person.

Question #4

How has your understanding of the concept of "forgiving yourself" changed? What role does *acceptance* play in releasing the self-bondage you have to past actions?

Question #5

Do you still believe there is anything in your past that you cannot be forgiven for by God? Is there anything that you repeatedly ask God to forgive you for, even though you understand that His forgiveness has already been given? As a group, are there merits to repeating this plea more than once? If you believe there are, what are those merits, and are they biblically sound?

Question #6

In what ways will you apply your new understanding of anger as a natural and physiological response in your processes for dealing with your own anger? What way will you apply this understanding when faced with the anger of another person?

Question #7

Do you think there is a situation in which anger is not rooted in fear? Discuss this as a group to see if you can peel away the onion on that situation and find the fear that initiates it (believe me, anger is *always* rooted in fear!)

Question #8

If someone has ever said, "I'll never forgive you for what you did," how do you plan to deal with that need for forgiveness now? Hint: the answer does not involve that other person.

Question #9

I have said that the absence of forgiveness is not about the Unforgiven, it is about the unforgiving. Are there examples of unforgiveness towards another in your life? How has that affected you? Do you still feel the pain and hurt? How would your life improve if you let go of that? What do you think you need to focus on in yourself to get to the point where you can forgive them?

Jim Melanson

Poet, programmer, procrastinator, sci-fi geek, coffee snob, actor, writer.

A devoted Christian, Jim is a quiet and thoughtful man who tends to think deeply, and act slowly. Much of this inner reflection and self-assessment shows up in his writing. "Capturing what truly motivates us," is how Jim describes his approach to both fiction and non-fiction. This author has a direct, and sometimes *in-your-face,* way of writing. He tries to always use conversational language and make complex ideas understandable.

Jim read his first novel by Laura Ingalls Wilder at the age of eight, and this began his love affair with the written word. Jim's first foray into personal writing, as a child, was poetry. These and other poetic scribblings provided the content for his first book, *I Apologize for Nothing*, published in April 2014.

Life, a child, a career with the Police Service, and a part-time business authoring software all got in the way of pursuing his desire to write. In 2013, Jim decided to pursue his creative yearnings, and he began writing for pleasure. Drawing on a solid work ethic from his experience authoring technical manuals and writing business proposals, Jim found writing for himself to be liberating and enjoyable. While working on his first fiction novel, he kept getting sidetracked by other ideas. He dusted off an old stage play he had written and published it under the title, *Mama's Slippers*, with the hopes of attracting production interest. In addition to non-fiction works on Christian topics, Jim also works on science fiction projects, including short stories and flash stories.

Originally hailing from the East Coast, Jim now lives just outside Cobourg, ON, with his two cats, Martin & Lewis.

End Notes

[1] Thomas, D. (Writer). (2016, February 25). The Caretaker (No. 78) [Television series episode]. In *The Blacklist*. New York, NY: NBC.

[2] AllAboutGod.com (n.d.). Definition for Forgiveness. Retrieved from http://www.allaboutgod.com/definition-for-forgiveness-faq.htm

[3] Fabrega, M. (2014, April 12). Five Powerful Ways to Forgive Those Who Hurt You. *Daring to Live Fully*. Retrieved from https://daringtolivefully.com/how-to-forgive

[4] Delio, I. (2010, January 30). *Christ in Evolution*. Logos Press: Idaho. p.167

[5] Wilson, D., Rev. (n.d.). God's Definition of Forgiveness. *The Journal of Greenville Presbyterian Theological Seminary,* 1-2. Retrieved from http://gpts.edu/resources/documents/katekomen/Forgiveness-1.pdf

[6] Jackson, W. (n.d.). Understanding Forgiveness. *Christian Courier*. Retrieved from https://www.christiancourier.com/articles/887-understanding-forgiveness

[7] Piper, J. (1994, March 20). As We Forgive Our Debtors: What Does Forgiveness Look Like? *desiringGod*. Retrieved from http://www.desiringgod.org/messages/as-we-forgive-our-debtors

[8] Willard, D. (2006). *The Great Omission: Reclaiming Jesus's Essential Teachings on Discipleship*. New York, NY: HarperOne, an imprint of HarperCollins.

[9] Toussaint, L. L., Owen, A. D., & Cheadle, A. (2011). Forgive to Live: Forgiveness, Health, and Longevity. *Journal of Behavioral Medicine,* 35(4), 375-386. doi:10.1007/s10865-011-9362-4

[10] Storms, S., Dr. (2011, May 4). Forgiveness: What It Is & What It Is Not. Retrieved from http://www.acts29.com/forgiveness-what-it-is-what-it-is-not/

[11] Ross, V. (2009, November 16). Forgotten Memories Linger in the Brain. *Science Line*. Retrieved from http://scienceline.org/2009/11/forgotten-memories-linger-in-the-brain/

[12] Reas, E. (2013, October 15). Important New Theory Explains Where Old Memories Go. *Scientific American.* Retrieved from https://www.scientificamerican.com/article/important-new-theory-explains-where-old-memories-go/

[13] Klimas, L. (2015, May 29). Scientists Have Figured Out How to Recover Forgotten Memories Still Lurking in the Brain. *The Blaze.* Retrieved from http://www.theblaze.com/news/2015/05/29/scientists-have-figured-out-how-to-recover-forgotten-memories-still-lurking-in-the-brain/

[14] Fitzgerald, M. (2013, April 22). Gone But Not Forgotten? The Mystery Behind Infant Memories. *Brain Connection.* Retrieved from http://brainconnection.brainhq.com/2013/04/22/gone-but-not-forgotten-the-mystery-behind-infant-memories/

[15] Petherbridge, L. (2012, July 19). What Forgiveness is NOT. Retrieved from http://www.crosswalk.com/faith/women/what-forgiveness-is-not.html

[16] Altrogge, M. (n.d.). 5 Things Forgiveness Doesn't Mean. Retrieved from http://www.biblestudytools.com/blogs/mark-altrogge/5-things-forgiveness-doesn-t-mean.html

[17] Morrison, T. (2014, October 02). The Real Danger of Unforgiveness. *Relevant Magazine.* Retrieved from http://archives.relevantmagazine.com/life/real-danger-unforgiveness

[18] Richmond, R. L., Ph.D. (n.d.). *Healing Emotional Wounds: Emotional Healing | Christian Catholic Healing Psychology.* Retrieved from http://www.chastitysf.com/healing.htm

[19] Warren, R. (2016). *The Purpose-Driven Life: What on Earth Am I Here For?* Grand Rapids, MI: Zondervan. p.148

[20] Clarke, S. (2016, July 8). Is Forgiveness A Sign Of Weakness In Leaders? *Leaderonomics.com.* Retrieved from https://leaderonomics.com/leadership/forgiveness-and-leadership

[21] Spurgeon, C. (1878). Sermon No. 1448. Sermon presented in Metropolitan Tabernacle, Newington (London). Retrieved from http://www.biblebb.com/files/spurgeon/1448.htm

[22] Lewis, C. S. (2005). *The Weight of Glory.* p.183. San Francisco: Harper.

[23] Meyer, J. (n.d.). The Poison of Unforgiveness. *Joyce Meyer*

Ministries. Retrieved from http://www.joycemeyer.org/articles/ea.aspx?article=the_poison_of_unforgiveness

[24] Tutu, D. (1999). *No Future Without Forgiveness (1st ed.).* Norwalk, CT: Easton Press. p.272

[25] Morrison, T. (2014, October 02). The Real Danger of Unforgiveness. *Relevant Magazine.* Retrieved from http://archives.relevantmagazine.com/life/real-danger-unforgiveness

[26] Door of Hope Counseling Center (2016, June 13). Forgiving Others – Releasing Yourself from the Past.

[27] Barnes, R., Pastor. (n.d.). The Danger of Unforgiveness! Retrieved from http://www.asoneministries.org/danger_of_unforgiveness

[28] Gemmell, D. (2007, May 30) What is Forgiveness. Retrieved from https://www.youtube.com/watch?v=SclcmVLS-Hw

[29] Dee, M. (2013, April 01). *Merri Dee, Life Lessons on Faith, Forgiveness & Grace.* Matteson, IL: Life to Legacy.

[30] Clinton, W. J. (2000). *William J. Clinton: 1999 (in two books)*: book 1-January 1 to June 30, 1999: book II-July 1 to December 31, 1999. Washington: U.S. Govt. Printing Office. p.27

[31] GotQuestions.Org (2017, January 20). Why did Jesus say "Father, forgive them" on the cross? Retrieved from https://www.gotquestions.org/Father-forgive-them.html

[32] Spurgeon, C. (1869, October 24). Sermon No. 897. Sermon presented in Metropolitan Tabernacle, Newington (London). Retrieved from https://www.blueletterbible.org/Comm/spurgeon_charles/sermons/0897.cfm

[33] Spurgeon, C. (1890, October 5). Sermon No. 2263. Sermon presented in Metropolitan Tabernacle, Newington (London). Retrieved from https://www.blueletterbible.org/Comm/spurgeon_charles/sermons/2263.cfm

[34] Johnson, L. (2015, June 22). The Deadly Consequences of Unforgiveness. *CBN News: The Christian Perspective.* Retrieved from http://www1.cbn.com/cbnnews/healthscience/2015/June/The-

Deadly-Consequences-of-Unforgiveness

[35] Johns Hopkins Medicine (n.d.). Forgiveness: Your Health Depends on It. Retrieved from http://www.hopkinsmedicine.org/health/healthy_aging/healthy_connections/forgiveness-your-health-depends-on-it

[36] Mayo Clinic (n.d.). Forgiveness: Letting go of grudges and bitterness. Retrieved from http://www.mayoclinic.org/healthy-lifestyle/adult-health/in-depth/forgiveness/art-20047692

[37] Krauss Whitborne, S., Ph.D. (2013, January 1). Live Longer by Practicing Forgiveness. *Psychology Today*. Retrieved from https://www.psychologytoday.com/blog/fulfillment-any-age/201301/live-longer-practicing-forgiveness

[38] Wade, N. G. (2010). Introduction to the Special Issue on Forgiveness in Therapy. *Journal of Mental Health Counseling, 32*(1), 1-4. Retrieved from http://transformationalchange.pbworks.com/f/Forgiveness in Therapy.pdf

[39] Wade, N. G., Hoyt, W. T., Kidwell, J. E. M., & Worthington, E. L., Jr. (2014, February). Efficacy of Psychotherapeutic Interventions to Promote Forgiveness: A Meta-Analysis. *Journal of Consulting and Clinical Psychology*. Advance online publication. doi: 10.1037/a0035268

[40] Lauer, A., Fr. (1996). Unforgiveness Is The Cause... *Presentation Ministries*. Retrieved from http://www.presentationministries.com/publications/UnforgivenessCause.asp

[41] *Deadly sin.* (n.d.). Retrieved from https://www.merriam-webster.com/dictionary/deadly%20sin

[42] Sinkewicz, R. E. (Ed.). (2006). *Evagrius of Pontus: The Greek Ascetic Corpus*. Oxford: Oxford University Press.

[43] Cassian, J. (1908) In *The Catholic Encyclopedia*. New York: Robert Appleton Company. Retrieved from New Advent: http://www.newadvent.org/cathen/03404a.htm

[44] Elwell, W. A. (Ed.). (1997). Baker's Evangelical Dictionary of Biblical Theology - Pride. In *Bible Study Tools*. Retrieved from http://www.biblestudytools.com/dictionary/pride/

[45] Cowen, G. (1991). Pride. In T. C. Butler (Ed.), *Holman Bible

Dictionary. Broadman & Holman. Retrieved http://www.studylight.org/dictionaries/hbd/p/pride.html
[46] Tarrants, T. A., III. (2011). Pride and Humility. *C.S. Lewis Institute*. Retrieved from http://www.cslewisinstitute.org/Pride_and_Humility_SinglePage
[47] Garland, T., Th.M., Th.D . (2015, March 1). Q93 : Can Pride be Good? Retrieved from http://www.spiritandtruth.org/questions/93.htm?x=x
[48] Miller, M. (2014, October 22). The deadly sin of price. *Canadian Mennonite*. 18-21. Retrieved from http://www.canadianmennonite.org/articles/deadly-sin-pride
[49] Tripp, P. (2011, July 06). Five "Benefits" of Unforgiveness (Then the Better Way). *desiringGod*. Retrieved from http://www.desiringgod.org/articles/five-benefits-of-unforgiveness-then-the-better-way
[50] Byrom Hartwell, M. (1999, May 3). The Role of Forgiveness in Reconstructing Society After Conflict. *The Journal of Humanitarian Assistance*. Retrieved from https://sites.tufts.edu/jha/archives/140
[51] TEDx Talks. (2015, October 28). Dolf Lundgren: On healing and forgiveness. [Video file]. Retrieved from https://www.youtube.com/watch?v=iNOE0dZpHcY
[52] Ford, M. T., Wang, Y., Jin, J., & Eisenberger, R. (2017, February 13). Chronic and Episodic Anger and Gratitude Toward the Organization: Relationships With Organizational and Supervisor Supportiveness and Extrarole Behavior. *Journal of Occupational Health Psychology*. doi:10.1037/ocp0000075
[53] Muller, R. J., Ph.D. (2009, March 26). Pathological Anger, Existentially Speaking. *Psychiatric Times*. Retrieved from http://www.psychiatrictimes.com/articles/pathological-anger-existentially-speaking
[54] Diamond, S. A., Ph.D. (2009, April 03). Anger Disorder: What It Is and What We Can Do About It [Web log post]. Retrieved from https://www.psychologytoday.com/blog/evil-deeds/200904/anger-disorder-what-it-is-and-what-we-can-do-about-it
[55] American Psychiatric Association. (2013). *Diagnostic and*

Statistical Manual of Mental Disorders, Fifth Edition. Arlington, VA: American Psychiatric Press.

[56] Treating Anger Disorders: Anger Management Treatment Program Options. (n.d.). Retrieved from http://www.psychguides.com/guides/treating-anger-disorders-anger-management-treatment-program-options/

[57] Staik, A. (2013). Expressing the Emotion of Anger, 2 of 3: Five Essential Things to Understand About Its Risks and Benefits. *Psych Central.* Retrieved from https://blogs.psychcentral.com/relationships/2013/01/expressing-the-emotion-of-anger-2-of-3-understanding-anger-its-risks-and-benefits/

[58] Staik, A. (2013). Expressing the Emotion of Anger, 1 of 3: Common Misconceptions About Anger. *Psych Central.* Retrieved from https://blogs.psychcentral.com/relationships/2013/01/expressing-the-emotion-of-anger-destructive-or-balancing-to-your-personal-life-and-relationships/

[59] Psych Central. (2016). Teenage Anger. *Psych Central.* Retrieved from https://psychcentral.com/lib/teenage-anger/

[60] Collingwood, J. (2016). Dealing with Anger Constructively. *Psych Central.* Retrieved from https://psychcentral.com/lib/dealing-with-anger-constructively/

[61] *Anger* [PDF]. (n.d.). Brenham, TX: Blinn College. Retrieved from https://www.blinn.edu/counseling/Anger.pdf

[62] Fleischer, R., & Medol, J. (n.d.). Fight or Flight: The Physiological Response. *Anger Alternatives.* Retrieved from http://www.anger.org/healthy-anger/fight-or-flight-the-physiological-response.html

[63] Vassar, G. (2011, February 01). How Does Anger Happen in the Brain? Retrieved from https://lakesideconnect.com/anger-and-violence/how-does-anger-happen-in-the-brain/

[64] Karmin, A. (2016, May 27). How Long Does the Fight or Flight Reaction Last? *Psych Central.* Retrieved from https://blogs.psychcentral.com/anger/2016/06/how-long-does-the-fight-or-flight-reaction-last/

[65] Berger, V., Dr. (2005). *Anger and Rage.* Retrieved from

http://www.psychologistanywhereanytime.com/emotional_problems_psychologist/pyschologist_anger.htm

[66] Seltzer, L. F., Ph.D. (2008, July 11). What Your Anger May Be Hiding. [Web log post]. Retrieved https://www.psychologytoday.com/blog/evolution-the-self/200807/what-your-anger-may-be-hiding

[67] Lemle, R. B., Ph.D. (2012, March 24). How Threat Emotions Cause Us To Misread Our Partner. [Web log post]. Retrieved from https://www.psychologytoday.com/blog/me-first-we-first/201203/how-threat-emotions-cause-us-misread-our-partner-4

[68] Stosny, S., Ph.D. (2008, December 29). Anger Problems: What They Say about You. [Web log post]. Retrieved from https://www.psychologytoday.com/blog/anger-in-the-age-entitlement/200812/anger-problems-what-they-say-about-you

[69] Smith, C. (2015). Principle 3: Anger is a response to injustice. *FireWorks*. Retrieved from https://www.k-state.edu/wwparent/courses/fireworks/principles/core3.html

[70] Beaumont, L. (n.d.). Anger: An Urgent Plea for Justice and Action. *Emotional Competency*. Retrieved from http://www.emotionalcompetency.com/anger.htm

[71] Bilodeau, L. (2001). Chapter 2: The Many Uses and Misuses of Anger. In *Responding to Anger: a Workbook* (pp. 31-32). Center City, MN: Hazelden Publishing.

[72] Warren, R., Pastor. (2014, May 21). *Conflict Resolution: Confront Someone In Love*. Retrieved from http://pastorrick.com/devotional/english/conflict-resolution-confront-someone-in-love

[73] Newmark, A., & Anderson, A. (2014). *Chicken Soup for the Soul: The Power of Forgiveness: 101 Stories about How to Let Go and Change Your Life*. Chapter 58. Cos Cob, CT: Chicken Soup for the Soul Publishing, LLC.

[74] Vaughan, H. (2012). The Great Sin [Web log post]. Retrieved from http://www.christlifemin.org/home/blog/articles/the-great-sin/

[75] Henry, M. (n.d.). Ephesians: Chapter IV. In *Matthew Henry's Commentary on the Whole Bible, Volume 6 (Acts to Revelation)* (pp. 1243-1244). Christian Classics Ethereal Library. Retrieved

from https://www.ccel.org/ccel/henry/mhc6.pdf

[76] Matthew Henry. (n.d.). Retrieved March 22, 2017, from http://www.ccel.org/ccel/henry

[77] Johnson, J. (2015, September 16). Is Frustration and Anger the Same Thing? *Anger management expert.* Retrieved from http://www.angermanagementexpert.co.uk/frustration-anger-same-thing.html

[78] Difference Between Frustration and Anger. (2013, February 06). Retrieved from http://www.differencebetween.com/difference-between-frustration-and-vs-anger/

[79] madisgram (2010, October 13). anger vs. frustration [Online forum comment]. Message posted to https://forums.psychcentral.com/1526282-post3.html

[80] De Botton, A. (2001). *The Consolations of Philosophy.* New York: Vintage Books. (p. 80).

[81] Berger, V., Dr. (2005). Frustration. Retrieved from http://www.psychologistanywhereanytime.com/emotional_problems_psychologist/pyschologist_frustration.htm

[82] Szasz, P. L., Szentagotai-Tatar, A., & Hofmann, S. G. (2011). The effect of emotion regulation on anger. *Behaviour Research and Therapy,* 49(2), 114-119. doi:DOI: 10.1016/j.brat.2010.11.011

[83] Scheve, T. (2009, June 22). Is there a link between exercise and happiness? *HowStuffWorks.com.* Retrieved from http://science.howstuffworks.com/life/exercise-happiness.htm

[84] Metro UK (2012, October 5). Gym rage: If you're feeling angry working out may not be the best idea. *Metro UK.* Retrieved from http://metro.co.uk/2012/10/05/gym-rage-if-youre-feeling-angry-working-out-may-not-be-the-best-idea-593529/

[85] Smith, J. C. (2013). Effects of Emotional Exposure on State Anxiety after Acute Exercise. *The Official Journal of the American College of Sports Medicine.* doi:DOI: 10.1249/MSS.0b013e31826d5ce5

[86] Reynolds, G. (2010, August 11). Phys Ed: Can Exercise Moderate Anger? *The New York Times.* Retrieved from https://well.blogs.nytimes.com/2010/08/11/phys-ed-can-exercise-moderate-anger/?_r=0

[87] Newton, M. (2012, April 24). Who Were Timothy And Titus?

Retrieved from https://bible.org/seriespage/who-were-timothy-and-titus

[88] Cole, S. J. (2013, April 15). Lesson 14: The Gentle Art of Correction (2 Timothy 2:23-26). Retrieved from https://bible.org/seriespage/lesson-14-gentle-art-correction-2-timothy-223-26

[89] Warren, R. (2014, May 21). Start The Healing By Revealing Your Hurt. [Web log post]. Retrieved from http://pastorrick.com/devotional/english/start-the-healing-by-revealing-your-hurt

[90] WebMD (2015). Overcoming Frustration and Anger - Topic Overview. Retrieved from http://www.webmd.com/mental-health/tc/overcoming-frustration-and-anger-topic-overview

[91] Beilock, S., Ph.D. (2012, September 19). The Power of Expressing Yourself. [Web log post]. Retrieved from https://www.psychologytoday.com/blog/choke/201209/the-power-expressing-yourself

[92] Khoshaba, D., Dr. (2012, May 29). Masks of Anger: The Fears That Your Anger May Be Hiding. [Web log post]. Retrieved from http://www.psychologyineverydaylife.net/2012/05/29/masks-of-anger-the-fears-that-your-anger-may-be-hiding/

[93] Heffner, C. L., Dr. (n.d.). *Chapter 3: Section 5: Freud's Structural and Topographical Model.* Retrieved from https://allpsych.com/psychology101/ego/

[94] Borghini, F., Garzia, F., Borghini, A., & Borghini, G. (2016). *The Psychology of Security, Emergency and Risk.* pp 9-11. Southampton: WIT Press

[95] Buber, M. (1999). *Martin Buber on Psychology and Psychotherapy: Essays, Letters, and Dialogue.* Syracuse, NY: Syracuse University Press.

[96] TEDx Talks. (2013, October 1). The power of forgiveness: Al Valdez at TEDxUCIrvine. [Video file]. Retrieved from https://www.youtube.com/watch?v=Vv-qg1Loc1Y

[97] Warnock, A. (2013, June 6). Should a Christian go to counseling with a secular therapist? [Web log post]. Retrieved from http://www.patheos.com/blogs/adrianwarnock/2013/06/should-a-christian-go-to-counseling-with-a-secular-therapist/

[98] Verghese, A. (2008). Spirituality and mental health. *Indian Journal of Psychiatry*, 50(4), 233-237. doi:10.4103/0019-5545.44742

[99] Stetzer, E. (2013, April). Mental Illness & Medication vs. Spiritual Struggles & Biblical Counseling [Web log post]. Retrieved from http://www.christianitytoday.com/edstetzer/2013/april/mental-illness-medication-vs-spiritual-struggles.html

[100] Boorstein, M. (2013, April 10). Suicide of star pastor Rick Warren's son sparks debate about mental illness. *Washington Post*. Retrieved from https://www.washingtonpost.com/local/suicide-of-megapastor-rick-warrens-son-sparks-debate-about-mental-illness/2013/04/10/322e4910-a148-11e2-9c03-6952ff305f35_story.html?utm_term=.5e0a8459dc44

[101] Lifeway Research (2014, September). Study of Acute Mental Illness and Christian Faith [PDF]. *Lifeway Research*. Retrieved from http://lifewayresearch.com/wp-content/uploads/2014/09/Acute-Mental-Illness-and-Christian-Faith-Research-Report-1.pdf

[102] Cox, B. (2013, December 30). What Every Pastor Needs to Know About Mental Illness. *ChurchLeaders.com*. Retrieved from http://churchleaders.com/pastors/pastor-how-to/171880-brandon-cox-every-pastor-needs-to-know-about-mental-illness.html

[103] Moussavi-Bock, D. (2012, June). A shift in perspective can change our attitudes and our outcomes. *The Learning Professional (formerly JSD)*, 33(3), 54. Retrieved from https://learningforward.org/docs/jsd-june-2012/scott333.pdf?sfvrsn=2

[104] Working Through Emotions: Peel Back the Layers of the Onion. (n.d.). [Web log post]. Retrieved from https://www.feelingmagnets.com/blogs/feeling-magnets/18815719-working-through-emotions-peel-back-the-layers-of-the-onion

[105] Swan, W. (2012, June 22). Emotional Layers - Peeling the Onion [Web log post]. Retrieved from http://stepupstepforward.blogspot.ca/2012/06/emotional-layers-peeling-onion.html

[106] Reddy, C. (2015, December 18). The Teacher Curse No One Wants to Talk About [Web log post]. Retrieved from https://www.edutopia.org/blog/the-curse-of-knowledge-chris-reddy

[107] Baum, D. (2013, May 07). Peeling Back the Layers. *Beyond Today*. Retrieved from https://www.ucg.org/beyond-today/peeling-back-the-layers

[108] Shankar, R. (n.d.). Don't be a football of other people's opinions. Retrieved from https://www.artofliving.org/2-dont-be-football-other-peoples-opinions

[109] Swindoll, C. R. (n.d.). Lamentations. Retrieved from https://www.insight.org/resources/bible/the-major-prophets/lamentations

[110] Henry, M. (n.d.). Lamentations: Chapter III. In *Matthew Henry's Commentary on the Whole Bible Volume IV (Isaiah to Malachi)* [PDF] (pp. 1286-1287). Christian Classics Ethereal Library. Retrieved from http://www.ccel.org/ccel/henry/mhc4.pdf

[111] Grimsrud, T. (n.d.). 2. Starting with self-understanding. [Web log post]. Retrieved from https://peacetheology.net/spirituality/2-starting-with-self-understanding/

[112] Herbert, W. (2010, October). Heuristics Revealed. *Association for Psychological Science*. Retrieved from http://www.psychologicalscience.org/observer/heuristics-revealed

[113] Reference.Com (n.d.). What are heuristics in psychology? Retrieved from https://www.reference.com/world-view/heuristics-psychology-7bbe46ad26ec0be2

[114] Chegg.Com. (n.d.). Cognitive Bias Lesson. Retrieved from http://www.chegg.com/homework-help/definitions/cognitive-bias-13

[115] Chegg (2016, March 14). Cognitive Biases | Psychology | Chegg Tutors. [Video File] Retrieved from https://www.youtube.com/watch?v=ycvEjU1Bx3o

[116] Taylor, J., Ph.D. (2011, July 18). Cognitive Biases vs. Common Sense. [Web log post]. Retrieved from https://www.psychologytoday.com/blog/the-power-prime/201107/cognitive-biases-vs-common-sense

[117] Program on Negotiation: Anchoring Effect. (n.d.). Retrieved from http://www.pon.harvard.edu/tag/anchoring-effect/

[118] Scopelliti, I., Morewedge, C. K., McCormick, E., Min, H. L., Lebrecht, S., & Kassam, K. S. (2015, April 24). Bias Blind Spot: Structure, Measurement, and Consequences. *Management Science,* 61(10), 2468-2486. Retrieved from http://pubsonline.informs.org/doi/abs/10.1287/mnsc.2014.2096

[119] Sherman, M., Ph.D. (2014, June 20). Why We Don't Give Each Other a Break. [Web log post]. Retrieved from https://www.psychologytoday.com/blog/real-men-dont-write-blogs/201406/why-we-dont-give-each-other-break

[120] Roese, N. J., & Vohs, K. D. (2012). Hindsight Bias [Abstract]. *Perspectives on Psychological Science*, 7(5). Retrieved from http://journals.sagepub.com/doi/full/10.1177/1745691612454303

[121] Nations, T. (2015, May 27). 7 Deadly Assumptions #5 – I Knew It All Along! [Web log post]. Retrieved from http://leadnet.org/7-deadly-assumptions-5-i-knew-it-all-along/

[122] Dvorsky, G. (2013, January 09). *The 12 cognitive biases that prevent you from being rational.* Retrieved from http://io9.gizmodo.com/5974468/the-most-common-cognitive-biases-that-prevent-you-from-being-rational

[123] Nations, T. (2015, June 04). 7 Deadly Assumptions #6 – The Overconfidence Effect. [Web log post]. Retrieved from http://leadnet.org/7-deadly-assumptions-6-the-overconfidence-effect/

[124] Cherry, K. (2017, January 31). *What Is the Projection Bias?* Retrieved from http://www.explorepsychology.com/projection-bias/

[125] Herbig, S. (2011, December 01). The Semmelweis Reflex – Lifting the Curtain of Normalcy. *IQS Research*. Retrieved from http://iqsresearch.com/the-semmelweis-reflex-lifting-the-curtain-of-normalcy/

[126] O'Toole, J., MD, MPH CEDS. (2014, May 02). The Semmelweis Reflex. [Web log post]. Retrieved from https://www.kartiniclinic.com/blog/post/the-semmelweis-reflex/

[127] Colino, S. (2016, October 5). Are Biases Hurting Your Health? *US News & World Report*. Retrieved from http://health.usnews.com/wellness/articles/2016-10-05/are-biases-hurting-your-health

[128] Empathy. (n.d.). *Psychology Today.* Retrieved from https://www.psychologytoday.com/basics/empathy

[129] Roth-Hanania, R., Davidov, M., & Zahn-Waxler, C. (2011). Empathy development from 8 to 16 months: early signs of concern for others. *Infant Behavior and Development*, 34(3), 447-458.

[130] Watchtower Magazine (2002, April 15). Empathy — Key to Kindness and Compassion. *Watchtower Magazine,* (p.24). Retrieved from http://wol.jw.org/en/wol/d/r1/lp-e/2002285

[131] Bergland, C. (2013, October 10). The Neuroscience of Empathy. [Web log post]. Retrieved from https://www.psychologytoday.com/blog/the-athletes-way/201310/the-neuroscience-empathy

[132] Freeland, L. (2016, February 18). Why Christians Should Show Less Sympathy and More Empathy. *Crosswalk.com.* Retrieved from http://www.crosswalk.com/faith/spiritual-life/why-christians-should-show-less-sympathy-and-more-empathy.html

[133] Ulus, L., Ph.D. (2015). Empathy and Forgiveness Relationship. *International Journal of Research in Humanities and Social Studies*, 2(8), 98-103. Retrieved from http://www.ijrhss.org/pdf/v2-i8/14.pdf

[134] McCullough, M.E., Worthington, E. L., & Rachal, K. C. (1997). Interpersonal forgiving in close relationships. *Journal of Personality and Social Psychology*, 73 (2):321-336.

[135] Konstam, V., Chernoff, M., & Deveney, S. (2001, October). Toward forgiveness: The role of shame, guilt, anger, and empathy. *Counseling and Values*, 46(1), 26–39.

[136] Macaskill, A., Maltby, J., & Day, L. (2012). Forgiveness of Self and Others and Emotional Empathy. *The Journal of Social Psychology*, 142(5), 663-665.

[137] Mayer, J. D., Ph.D. (2009, September 21). What Emotional Intelligence Is and Is Not. [Web log post]. Retrieved from https://www.psychologytoday.com/blog/the-personality-analyst/200909/what-emotional-intelligence-is-and-is-not

[138] Mayer, J. D., Ph.D. (2014, May 6). Is Personal Intelligence Important? [Web log post]. Retrieved https://www.psychologytoday.com/blog/the-personality-analyst/201405/is-personal-intelligence-important

[139] Tibbits, D., Dr., & Halliday, S., Ph.D. (2008). *Forgive to Live: How Forgiveness Can Save Your Life*. Nashville: Thomas Nelson.
[140] Vivyan, C., RMN, RGN, Dip Cognitive Therapy, D.Hyp, GQHP (NMC, BABCP, GHR). (n.d.). The Helicopter View. [Web log post]. Retrieved from https://www.getselfhelp.co.uk/helicopter.htm
[141] Dincalci, J., Dr. (2011, June 9). *How to Forgive When You Can't: The Breakthrough Guide to Free Your Heart & Mind*. Ruah Press.
[142] Myss, C. M., & Shealy, C. N., Md. (1999). *The Creation of Health: The Emotional, Psychological, and Spiritual Responses that Promote Health and Healing*. London: Bantam.
[143] Seltzer, L. F., Ph.D. (2016, February 23). Anger: When Adults Act Like Children-and Why. [Web log post]. Retrieved from https://www.psychologytoday.com/blog/evolution-the-self/201602/anger-when-adults-act-children-and-why
[144] Den Haan, D., Rev. (2010, March 17). I just can't forgive myself. Sermon presented in Fairway Christian Reformed Church, Jenison, Michigan. Retrieved from https://www.crcna.org/resources/church-resources/reading-sermons/i-just-cant-forgive-myself
[145] Thomas, R. (2013, March 16). The Danger of Forgiving Yourself. Retrieved from http://rickthomas.net/the-danger-of-forgiving-yourself/
[146] Deis, R. (2015, March 15). A little learning is a dangerous thing. Retrieved from http://www.thisdayinquotes.com/2010/05/little-learning-is-dangerous-thing.html
[147] Morelock, B. (2011, December 05). Sipping from the Pierian Spring or, the Anatomy of Humility. Retrieved from http://www.classicalmpr.org/story/2011/12/02/sipping-from-the-pierian-spring
[148] Stewart, W. (2005). *An A-Z of Counselling Theory and Practice*. (p.223) Cheltenham, UK: Nelson Thornes.
[149] Bohlin, S. (2012, March 13). Forgive Myself? [Web log post]. Retrieved from http://blogs.bible.org/engage/sue_bohlin/forgive_myself_

[150] Vernick, L. (n.d.). When You Can't Forgive Yourself [Web log post]. Retrieved from http://www.biblestudytools.com/blogs/association-of-biblical-counselors/when-you-can-t-forgive-yourself.html

[151] Spurgeon, C. (1896, June 7). Sermon No. 2468. Sermon presented at the Metropolitan Tabernacle, Newington (London). Retrieved from https://www.blueletterbible.org/Comm/spurgeon_charles/sermons/2468.cfm?a=800019

[152] Swindoll, C. R. (n.d.). Galatians. Retrieved from https://www.insight.org/resources/bible/the-pauline-epistles/galatians

[153] Churches of Galatia [PDF]. (n.d.). Sacramento: First Slavic Evangelical Baptist Church of Sacramento. Retrieved from http://fsebc.org/wp-content/uploads/2014/03/Churches-in-Galatia_Eng.pdf

[154] United States Conference of Catholic Bishops (n.d.) The letter to the Galatians. Retrieved from http://www.usccb.org/bible/galatians/0

[155] Spurgeon, C. (1857, August 9). Sermon No. 145. Sermon presented at the Music Hall, Royal Surrey Gardens, Newington (London). Retrieved from http://www.spurgeon.org/sermons/0145.php

[156] Swindoll, C.R. (n.d.). Lamentations. Retrieved from https://www.insight.org/resources/bible/the-major-prophets/lamentations

[157] Britton, D. MFT (n.d.). The Bible Shows The Power in Humility. [Web log post]. Retrieved from https://www.dougbrittonbooks.com/onlinebiblestudies-selfworthandrespect/meaningofhumilityinthebible-humbleinbible/

[158] Brewer, J. (2011, October 12). The Sin You Can't Quit: Examining our misconceptions about habitual sin—and how to truly break it. *Relevant*. Retrieved from http://archives.relevantmagazine.com/god/deeper-walk/features/27020-the-sin-you-cant-quit

[159] Ingersoll-Dayton, B., Torges, C., & Kraus, N. (2010). Unforgiveness, Rumination, and Depressive Symptoms among

Older Adults [Abstract]. *Aging Mental Health*, 14(4), 439-449. doi:10.1080/13607860903483136

[160] Borschel-Dan, A. (2016, December 8). Holocaust survivor preaches forgiveness of Nazis as 'ultimate revenge'. *The Times of Israel*. Retrieved from http://www.timesofisrael.com/holocaust-survivor-preaches-forgiveness-of-nazis-as-ultimate-revenge/

[161] TEDx Talks. (2015, June 23). Sammy Rangel: The power of forgiveness [Video file]. Retrieved from https://www.youtube.com/watch?v=iOzJO6HRIuA

[162] TEDx Talks. (2013, November 23). Colleen Haggerty: Forgiving the unforgiveable. [Video file]. Retrieved from https://www.youtube.com/watch?v=FE7TaUG3qQI

[163] TEDx Talks (2015, December 22). Rachel King: The 'F' Word: Forgivness as a Way Forward. [Video File]. Retrieved from https://www.youtube.com/watch?v=iCkrS6k364U

[164] TEDx Talks. (2011, November 28). Dr. Chuck Sandstrom: Forgiveness as a Way of Life. [Video file]. Retrieved from https://www.youtube.com/watch?v=Wlw1SFGtjUc

[165] The Forgiveness Project (2016, August 2). Anne-Marie Cockburn (England). Retrieved from http://theforgivenessproject.com/stories/anne-marie-cockburn-england/

[166] The Forgiveness Project. (2016, October 18). Christopher Emmanuel (Canada). Retrieved from http://theforgivenessproject.com/stories/christopher-emmanuel-canada/

[167] The Forgiveness Project (2017, January 23). Margot Van Sluytman (Canada). Retrieved March from http://theforgivenessproject.com/stories/margot-van-sluytman-canada/

[168] The Forgiveness Project (2010, March 29). Katy Hutchison & Ryan Aldridge (Canada). Retrieved from http://theforgivenessproject.com/stories/katy-hutchison-ryan-aldridge-canada/

[169] TEDx Talks. (2013, June 10). Katy Hutchison: Restorative Practices to Resolve Conflict/Build Relationships [Video file]. Retrieved from https://www.youtube.com/watch?v=wcLuVeHlrSs

[170] Sugimoto, M. (2010). Woman who killed baby in DUI crash tearfully apologizes at sentencing. *Hawaii News Now*. Retrieved from http://www.hawaiinewsnow.com/story/13631475/big-island-woman

[171] Warren, L. (2014, June 11). Incredible moment mother of girl, 13, who was accidentally shot dead on school bus HUGS her daughter's killer in court after he was spared jail. *Mail Online*. Retrieved from http://www.dailymail.co.uk/news/article-2655057/Incredible-forgiveness-mother-girl-13-accidentally-shot-dead-school-bus-hugs-killer-court-spared-jail.html

[172] Ovalle, D. (2016, February 9). Miami teen who accidentally shot classmate joins victim's mom in talk to students. *Miami Herald*. Retrieved from http://www.miamiherald.com/news/local/community/miami-dade/homestead/article59381108.html

[173] Mail Online (2015, June 4). The incredible moment forgiving husband HUGGED the motorist, 23, who killed his cyclist wife while distracted by her phone. *Mail Online*. Retrieved from http://www.dailymail.co.uk/news/article-3111009/No-cellphone-2-years-driver-fatal-bike-crash.html

[174] FOX 47 News (2015, June 5) Man Hugs Driver Who Killed His Wife [Video File]. Retrieved from https://www.youtube.com/watch?v=8kVsXuN6Wvs

[175] Greig, A. (2014, May 16). Widow's incredible moment of forgiveness: Sobbing woman went to court so she could HUG the woman who killed her husband in horror crash as she was sentenced. *Mail Online*. Retrieved http://www.dailymail.co.uk/news/article-2630090/Widow-hugs-woman-killed-husband-sentenced-court.html

[176] CBC (2017, January 13). A drunk driver apologizes to the family of the person he killed. Retrieved from http://www.cbc.ca/radio/outintheopen/sorry-states-1.3934035/a-drunk-driver-apologizes-to-the-family-of-the-person-he-killed-1.3934062

[177] Bonner, D. (2015, May 13). Renee Napier and Eric Smallridge: An Incredible Story of Grace, Forgiveness and Repentance in Florida [Web log post]. Retrieved from

https://wonderingeagle.wordpress.com/2015/05/13/renee-napier-and-eric-smallridge-an-incredible-story-of-grace-forgiveness-and-repentance-in-florida/

[178] Blair, L. (2015, December 2). Hours Before She Was Fatally Shot, Pastor's Wife Amanda Blackburn Wrote Love Letter to Jesus. Retrieved from http://www.christianpost.com/news/amanda-blackburn-pastor-wife-killed-love-letter-jesus-151472/#44TFpSjstlvXcVx1.99

[179] Schwarzwalder, R., FRC. (2015, December 14). Meet the Christians Who Choose to Forgive the People Who Murdered Their Loved Ones. Retrieved from http://www.charismanews.com/opinion/53716-meet-the-christians-who-choose-to-forgive-the-people-who-murdered-their-loved-ones

[180] Ruiz, R. (2013, September 19). How do you forgive a killer? A mother moves past tragedy. *TODAY.com*. Retrieved from http://www.today.com/news/how-do-you-forgive-killer-mother-moves-past-tragedy-4B11203330

[181] Fogle, A., & Grosmaire, K. (2016, July 14). I Forgave My Daughter's Killer. *Good Housekeeping.* Retrieved from http://www.goodhousekeeping.com/life/inspirational-stories/a39313/kate-grosmaire-conor-mcbride-forgive-daughters-killer/

[182] Bailey, E. (2013, November 7). Catastrophizing. *Health Central.* Retrieved from http://www.healthcentral.com/anxiety/c/1443/164015/catastrophizing/

[183] Schreiner, M. (2016, December 1). Catastrophizing And Anxiety. *Evolution Counselling.* Retrieved from https://evolutioncounseling.com/catastrophizing-and-anxiety/

[184] White, B. (2011, August 01). Catastrophizing: Finding a Sense of P.E.A.C.E. *Chipur,* Retrieved from http://chipur.com/catastrophizing-finding-a-sense-of-peace/

www.ingramcontent.com/pod-product-compliance
Lightning Source LLC
Chambersburg PA
CBHW061319040426
42444CB00011B/2709